CAPY ROAD
The Pursuit of Capyness 2:
A Happier Capybara Coloring Book

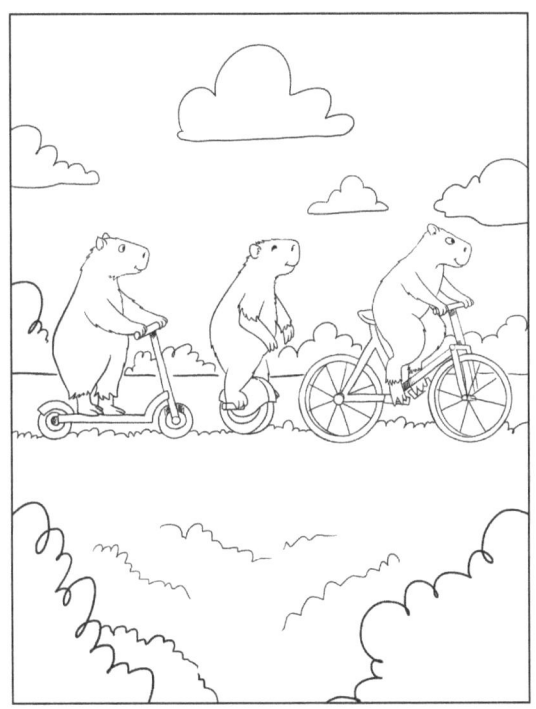

Dr. Jonathan Terry

Dr. Jonathan Terry
Walnut, CA
United States
2020

Capy Road - The Pursuit of Capyness 2: A Happier Capybara Coloring Book

Copyright © 2020 by Dr. Jonathan Terry

All rights reserved. No part of this book may be reproduced or transmitted in any form or by any means without written permission.

ISBN: 9798551863038

Names, characters, events, and incidents are the products of the editor's imagination; any resemblance to actual images, persons, animals, or actual events is purely coincidental.

Proceeds from the sales of this coloring book may be used to fund mental health initiatives at the discretion of the editor. For more information, please visit www.mycapybara.com.

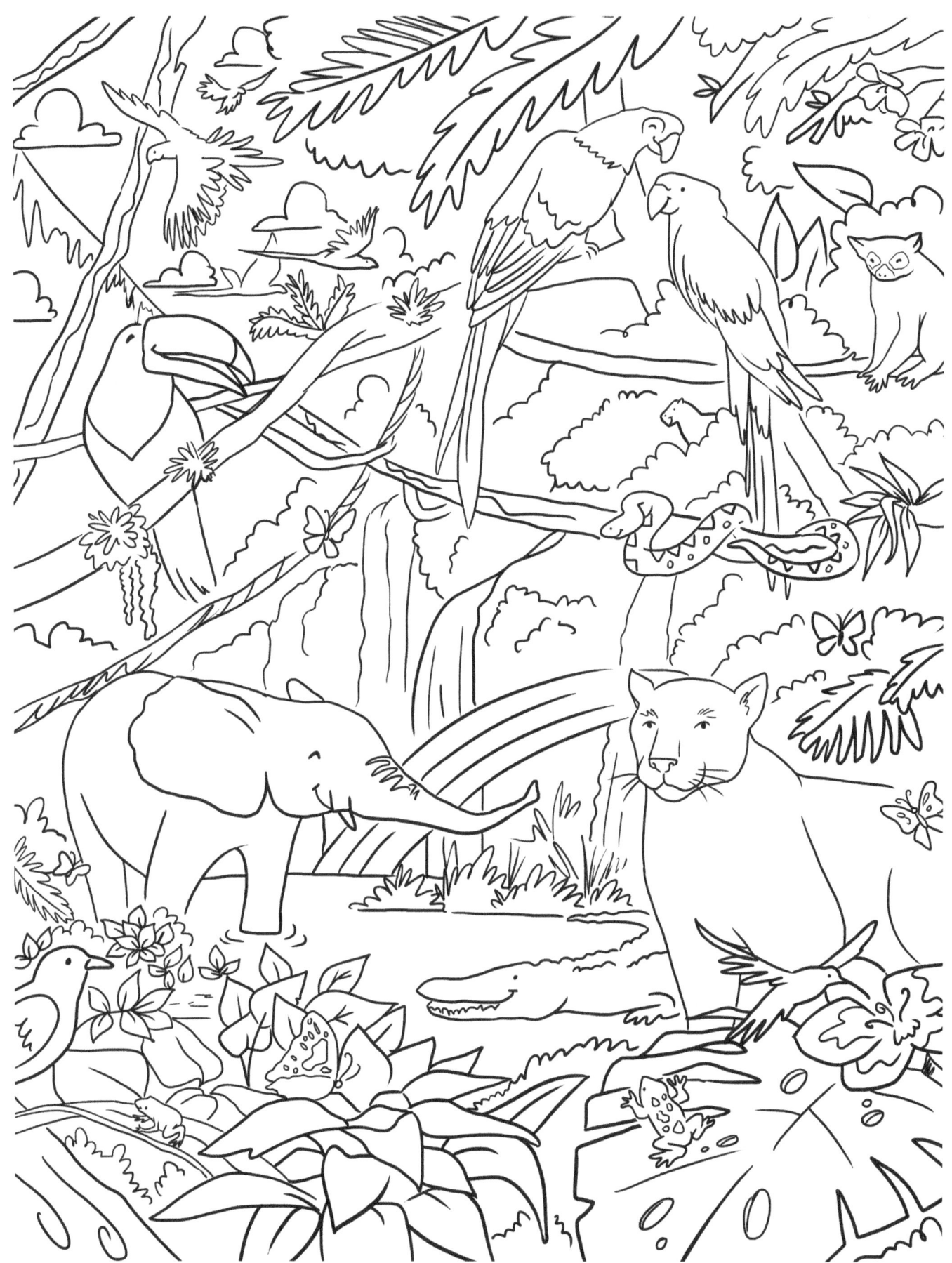

Wow, what a journey we've had with our educational coloring books so far!

We started in South America with the humble capybara.

We flew to Asia for some stup-pandous red pandas.

A quick teleport to North America took us to meet the Impossible opossum.

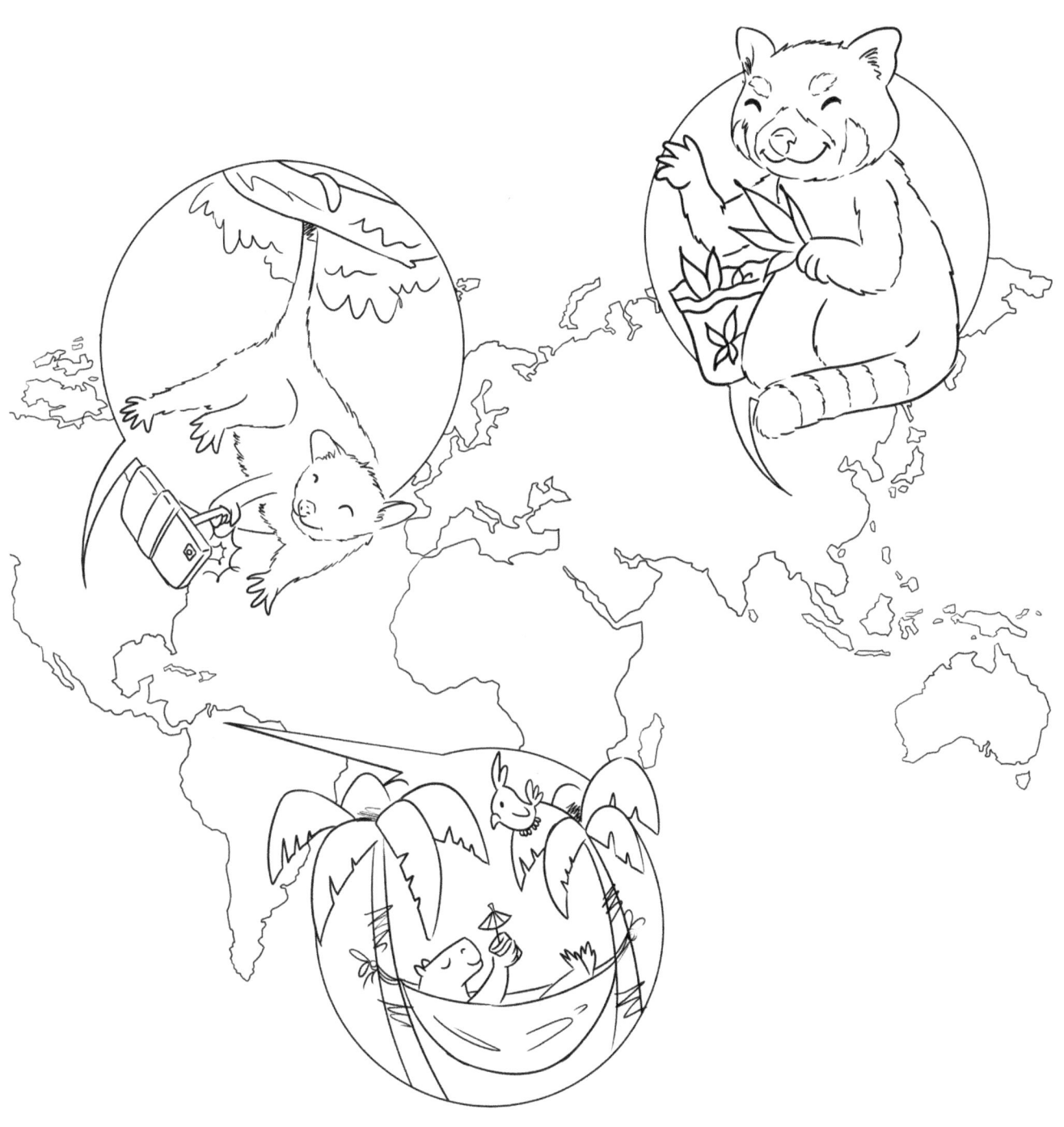

And what friends we've made along the way!

The Pursuit of Capyness has traveled to 6 continents (it's too cold in Antarctica for capybaras!), and your amazing coloring has shown up at weddings, graduations, art shows, in hospitals, in shelters, and on social media.

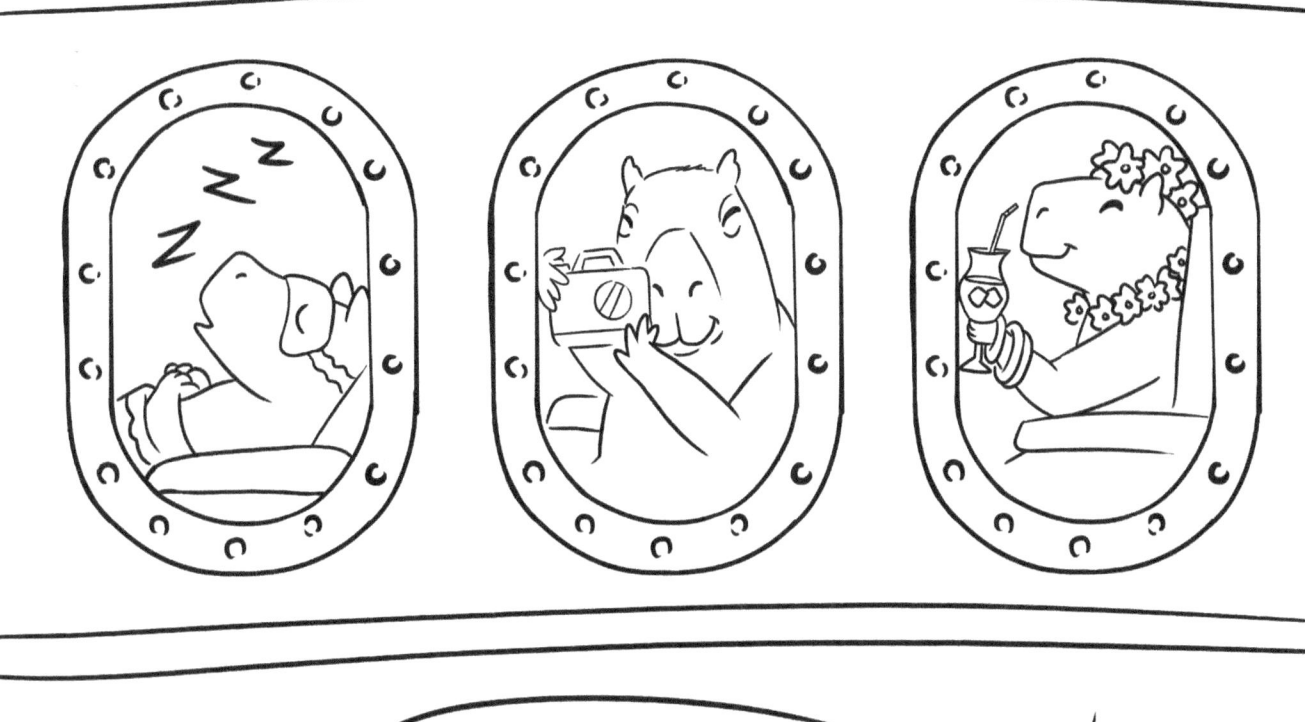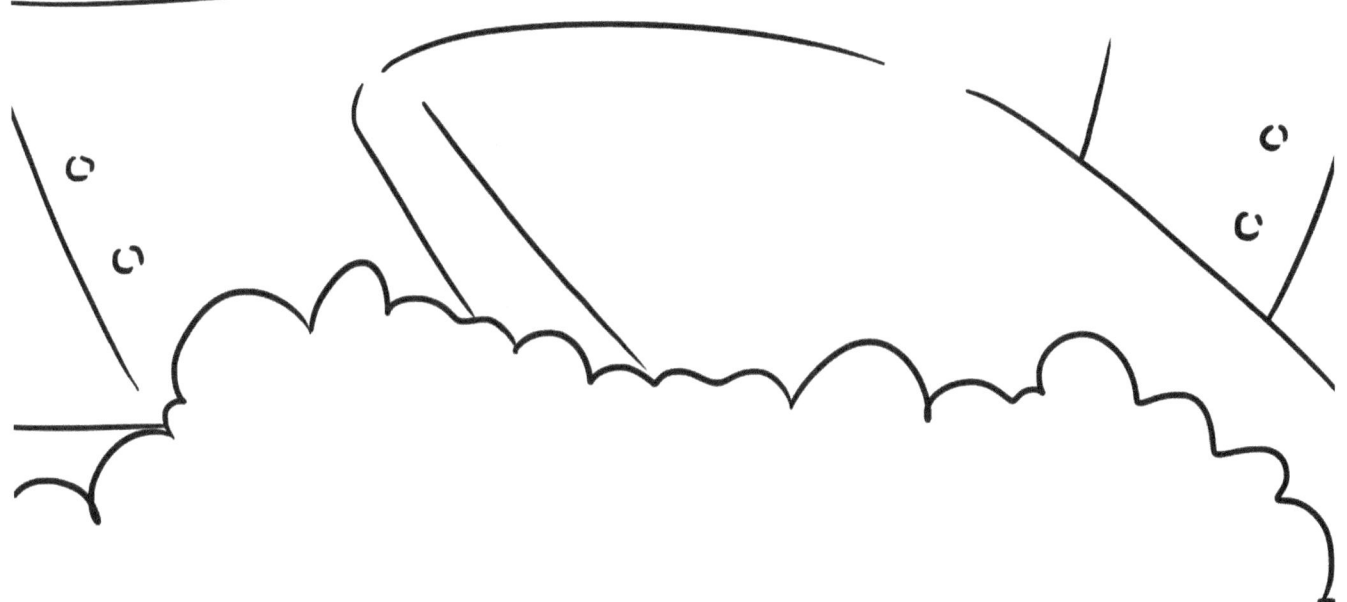

Coloring has even helped some at times of distress -- at times of loss, sadness, or feeling unwell.

If coloring has impacted your life, this page is for you. If you bought this book, rest assured that sales go toward helping other people who are struggling.

Coloring is a *feel-good* activity!

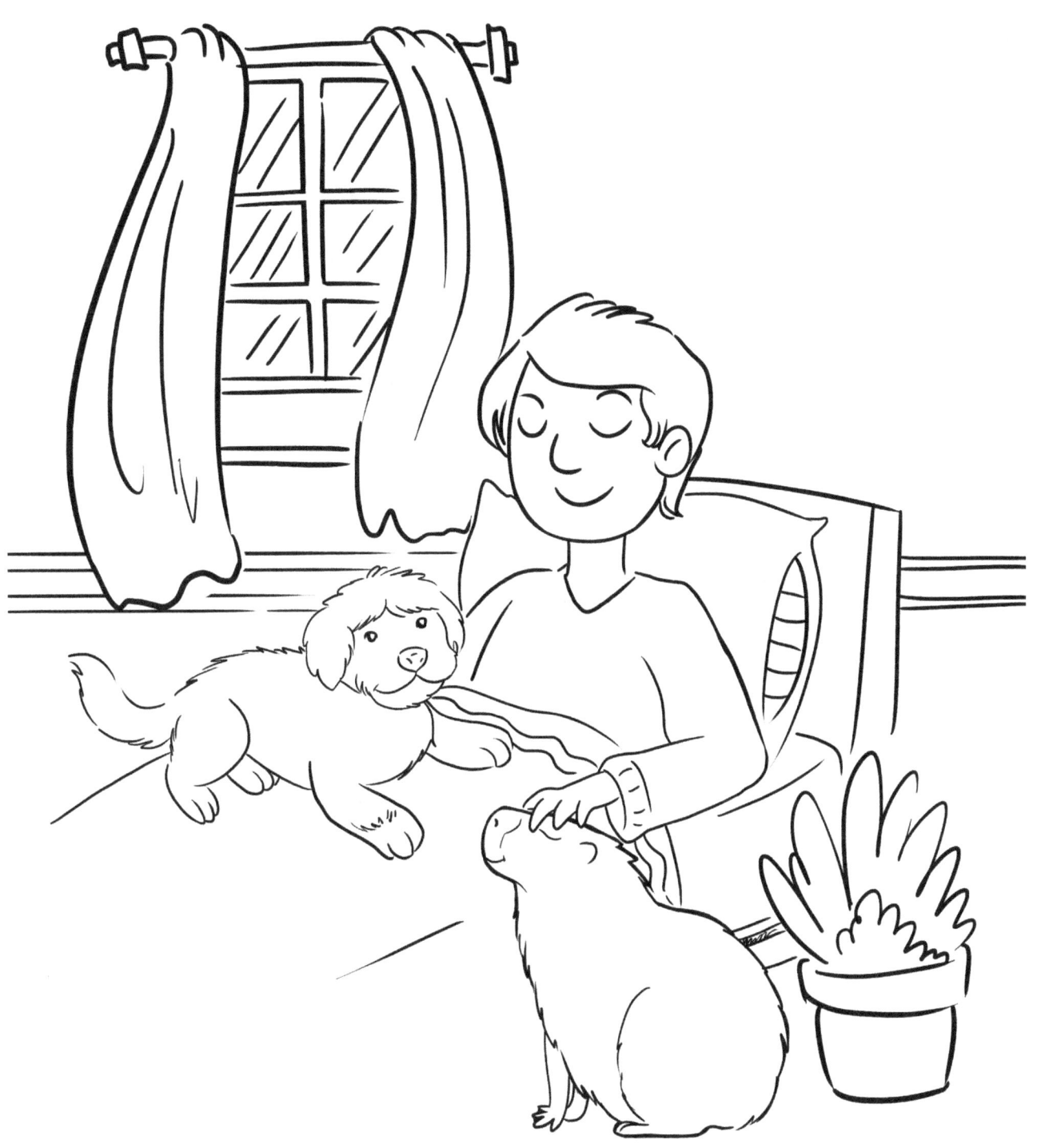

On our fourth book, we've also partnered with our favorite coloring book artist and capybara lover, Desiree Albarran!

Desiree is one of our international friends who has helped with all of the books so far. She lives in Colombia, not too far from the capybaras! If you have any questions about capybaras, you can go to Colombia and ask her. Tell her the coloring book sent you.

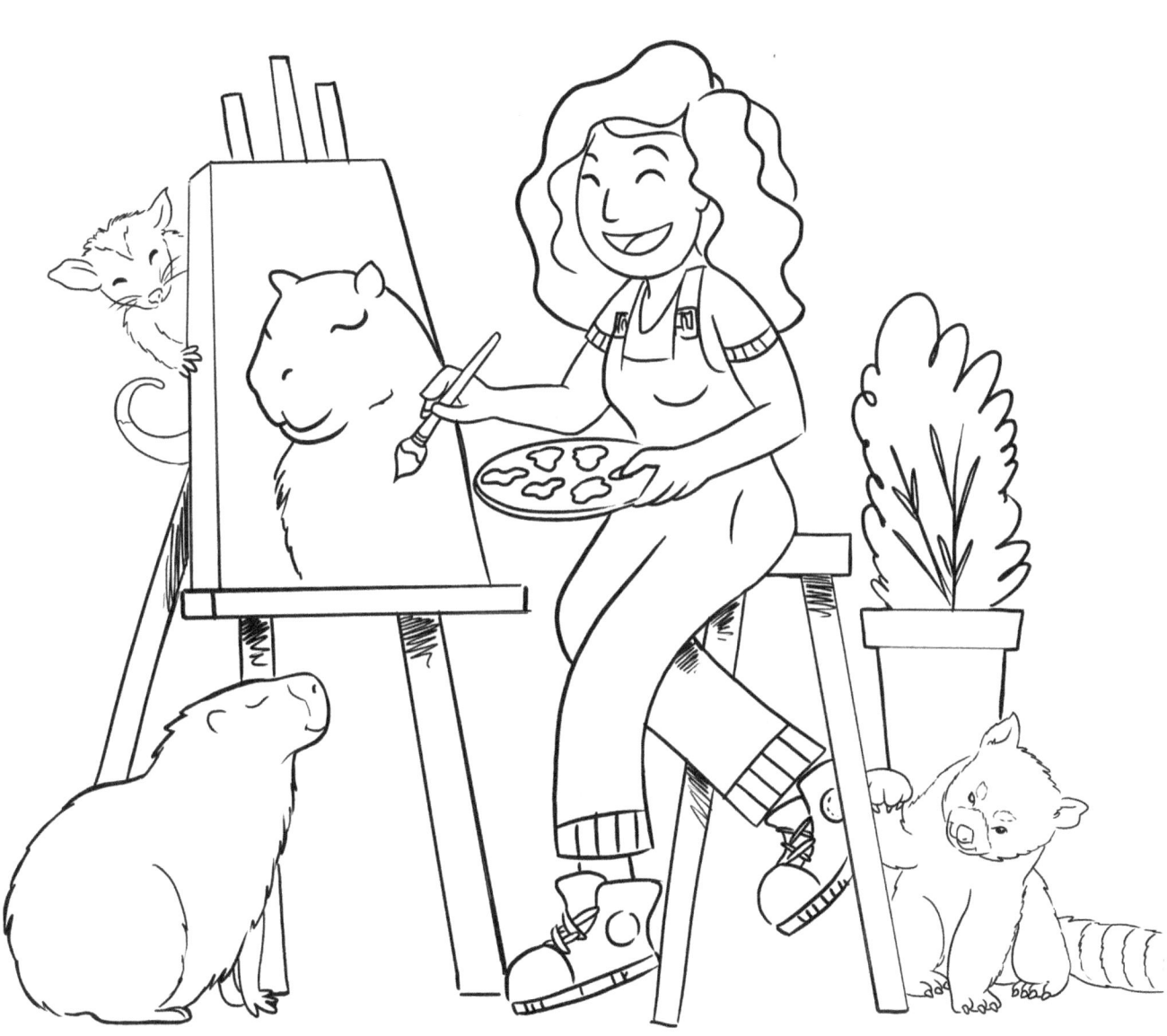

Well, that's enough background.

Good thing we're all caught up now!

Let's put on our explorer outfits and head to South America in search of the Holy Grail and to meet some *ratones grandes* !

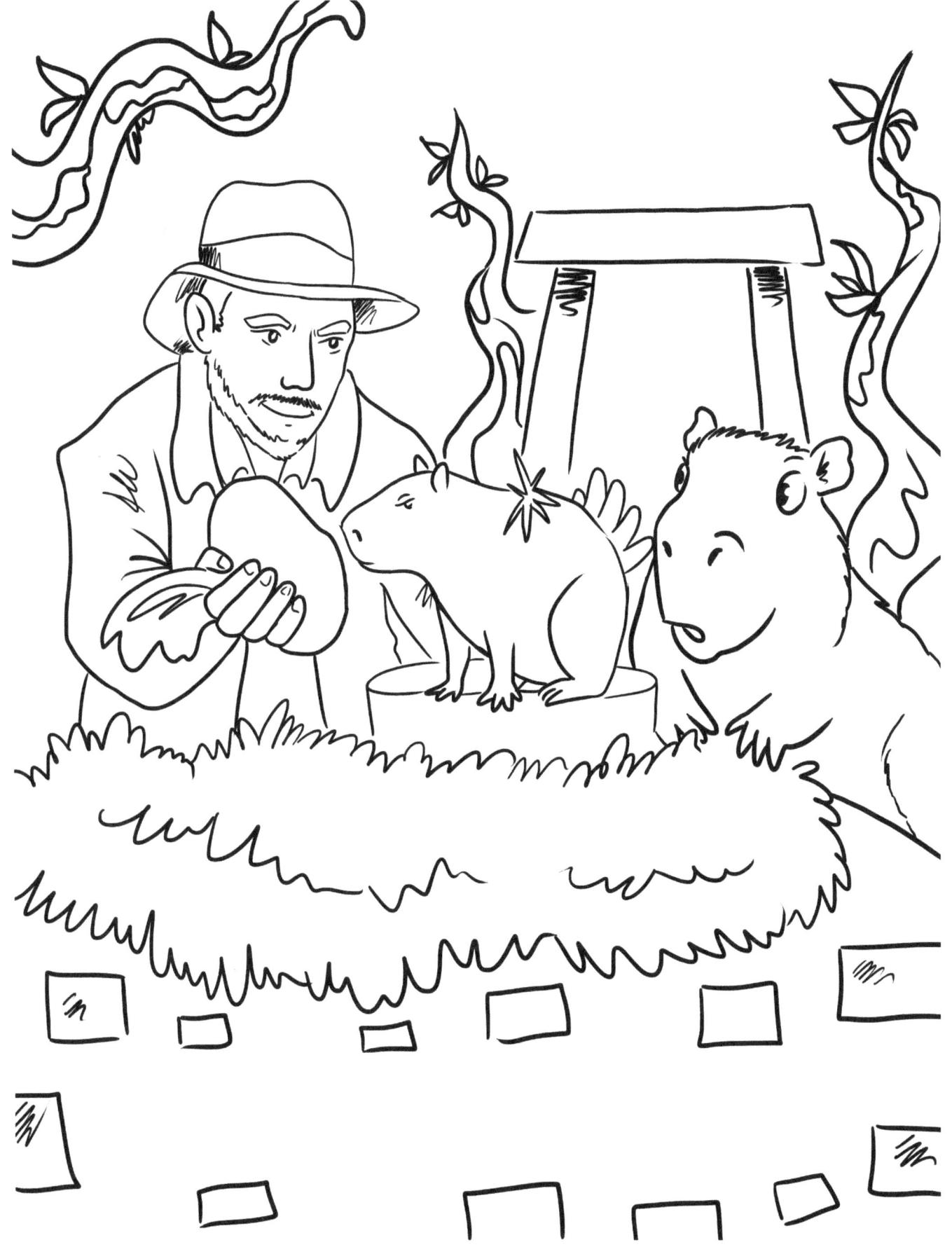

Wow, there are capybaras almost everywhere in South America!

I knew they'd be a lot of places, but I wasn't expecting them at the baggage claim...

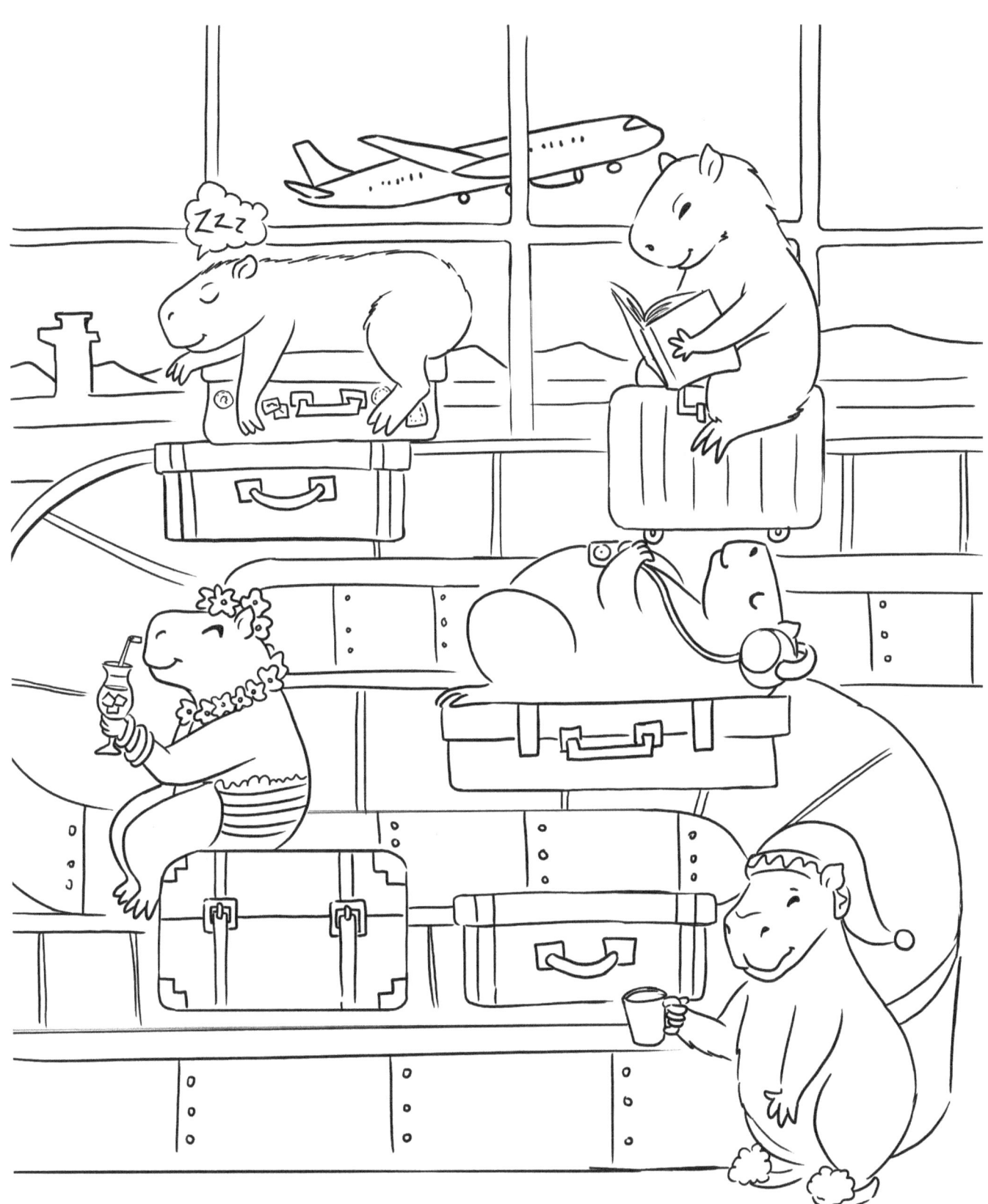

Capybaras can pretty much go where they want. After all, they are the LARGEST rodent on Earth.

Adults can weigh about 50kg (~110 pounds) and can be 120cm (~4ft) tall when they are trying to be really tall.

Why would a capybara stand on her hind legs? Funny you should ask…

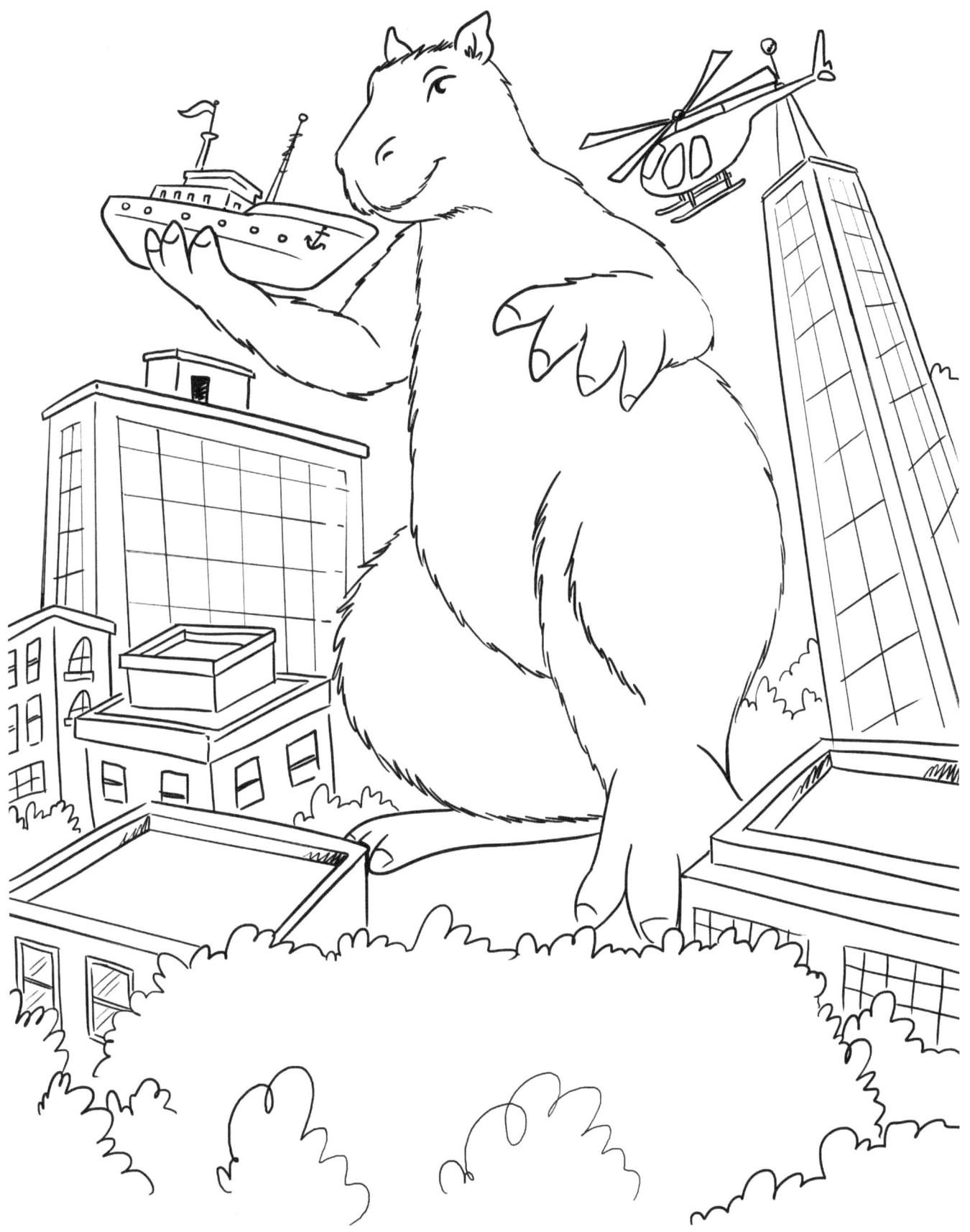

The real place the capybara excels, though, is near the water.

They love to live in forests near rivers and lakes.

You might even see a capybara swimming in the summer Olympics!

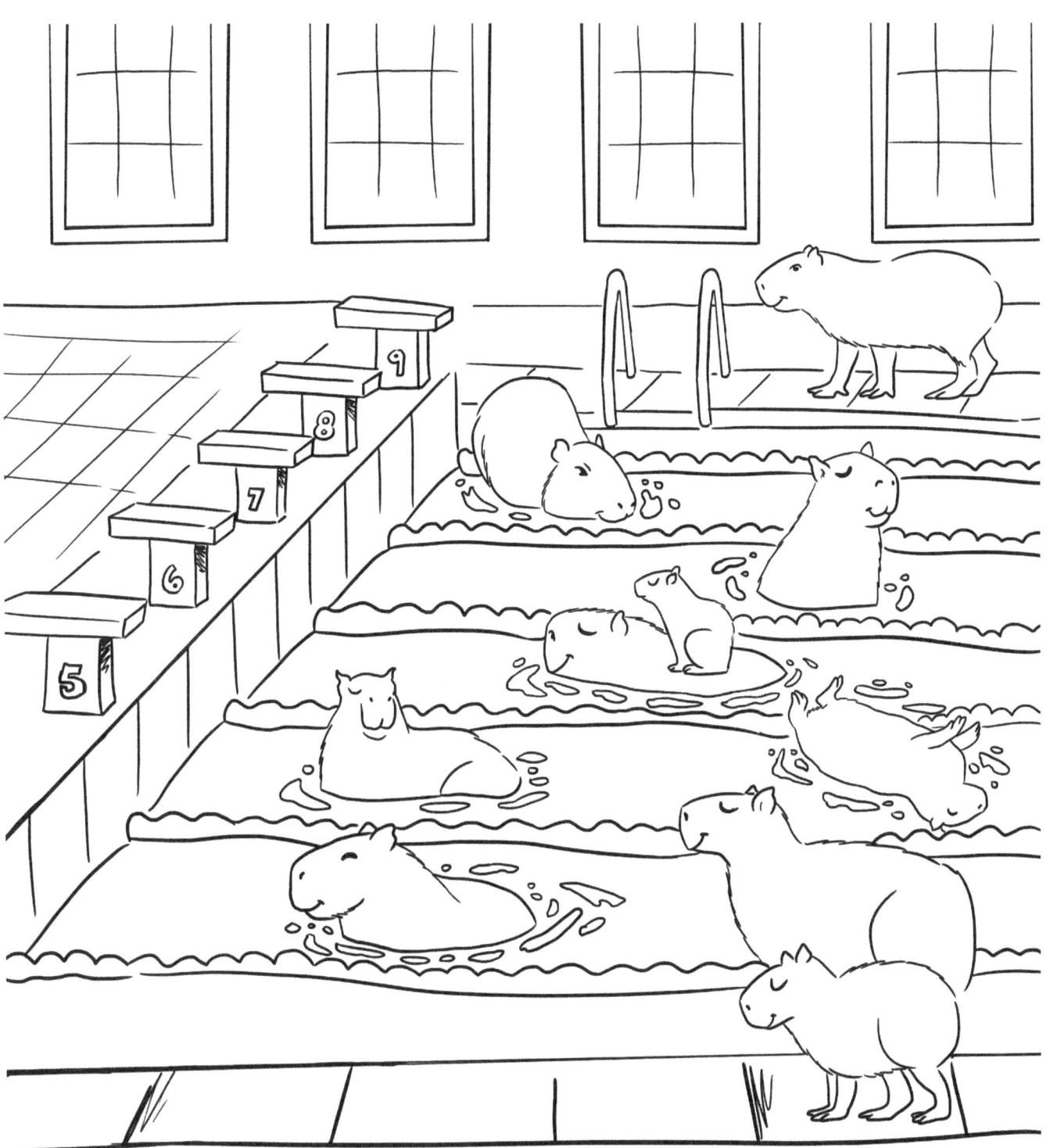

Is that a hippopotamus in that river?

From the nose and tiny, oval ears, it sure looks like it.

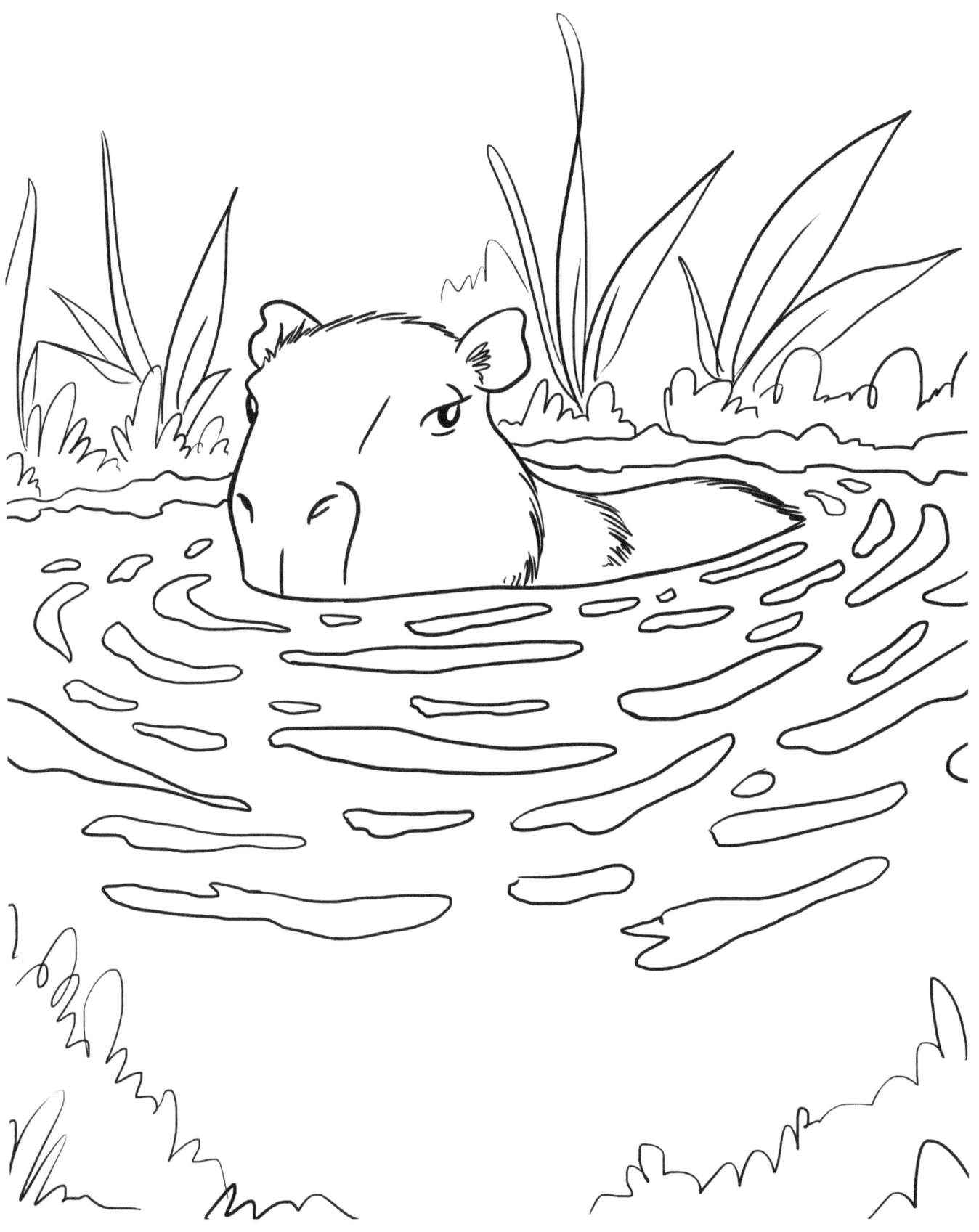

South America is home to the capybara's two closest living relatives:

the rock cavy and the guinea pig.

I think we can agree that the capybara is a guinea BIG.

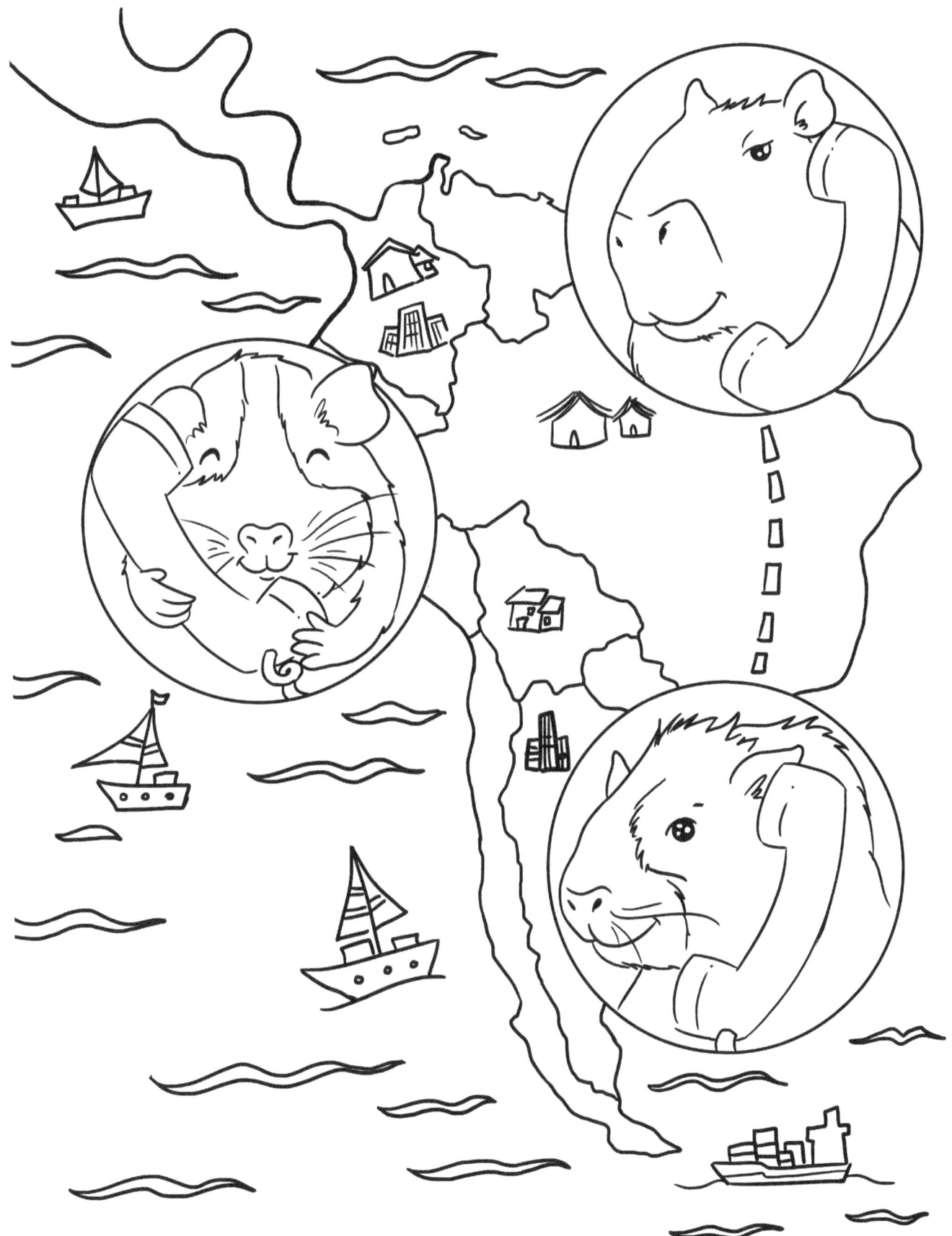

The capybara is not to be confused with the chupacabra!

The chupacabra ("goat-sucker") is a legendary, mythical creature in the Americas. They are scary.

Capybaras are not scary at all!

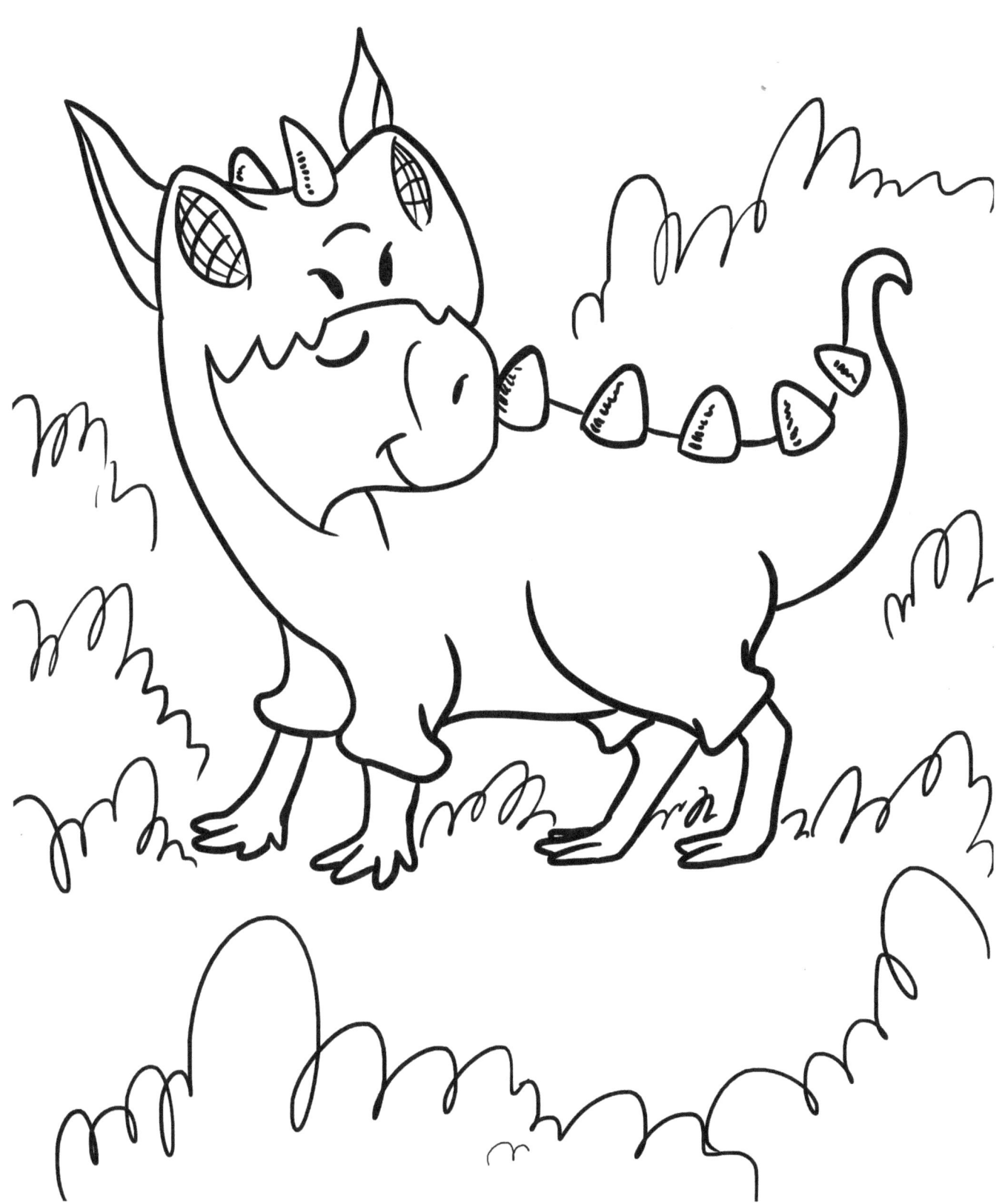

Speaking of big, scary animals, did you know there used to be a rodent even BIGGER than the capybara?!

2 to 4 million years ago, there was a 908kg (~1 ton) rodent that was about 3 meters (~10 feet) long.

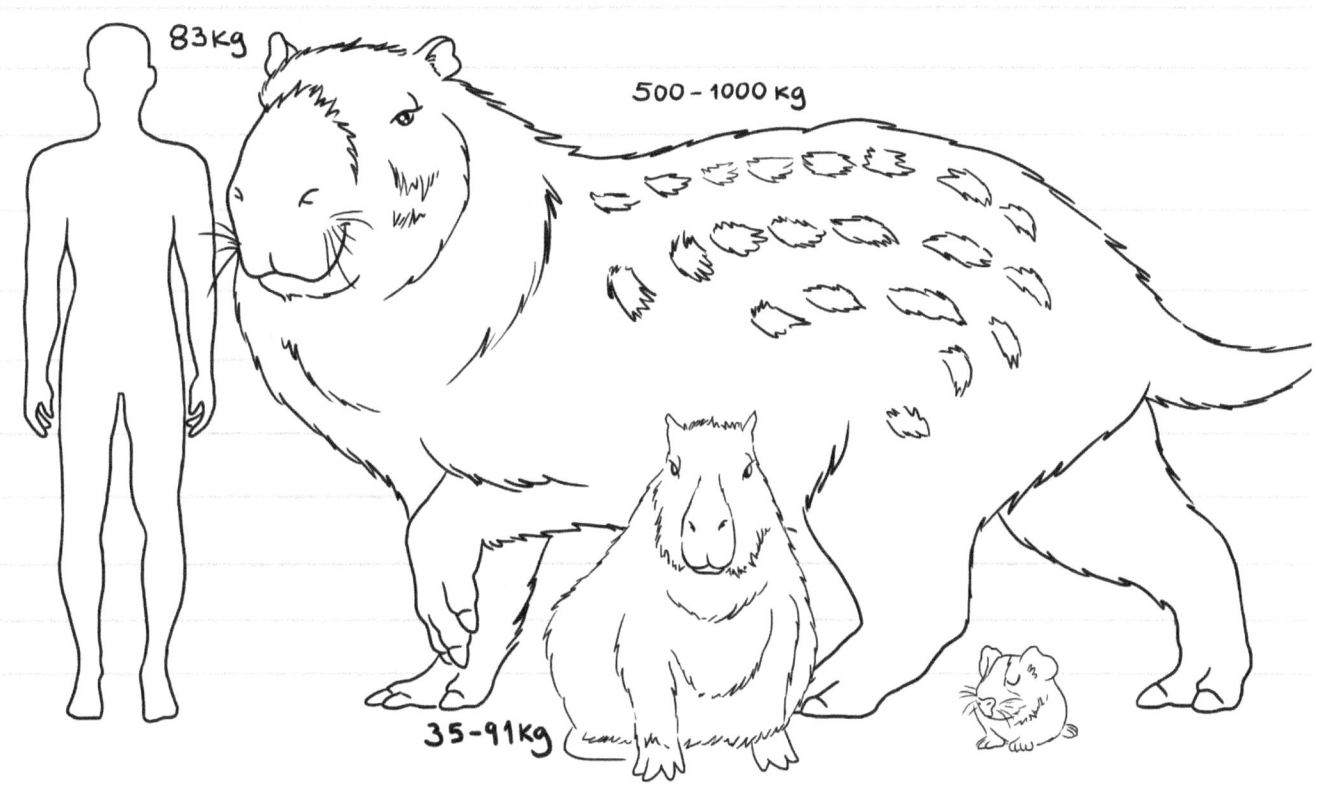

Spider pig…Spider pig…just kidding!

We meant to say *water pig*! This is the translation for *Hydrochoerus hydrochaieris*, the scientific name for the capybara.

Most capybaras don't know this when asked.

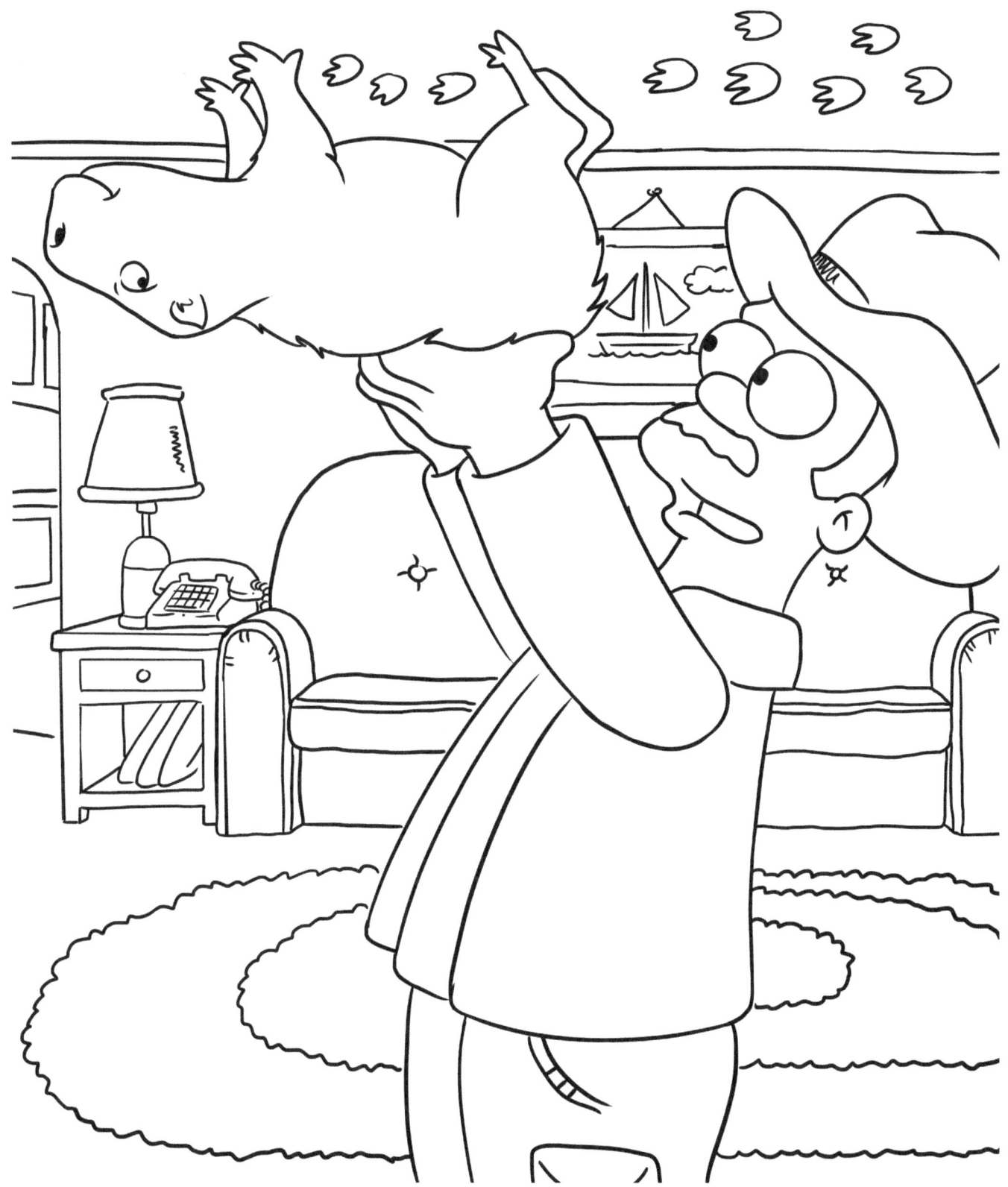

Wow, put some lotion on that water pig!

Capybaras have super dry skin and fur even though they spend all day at the mud spa.

Capybaras love mud! And spas. But mostly mud.

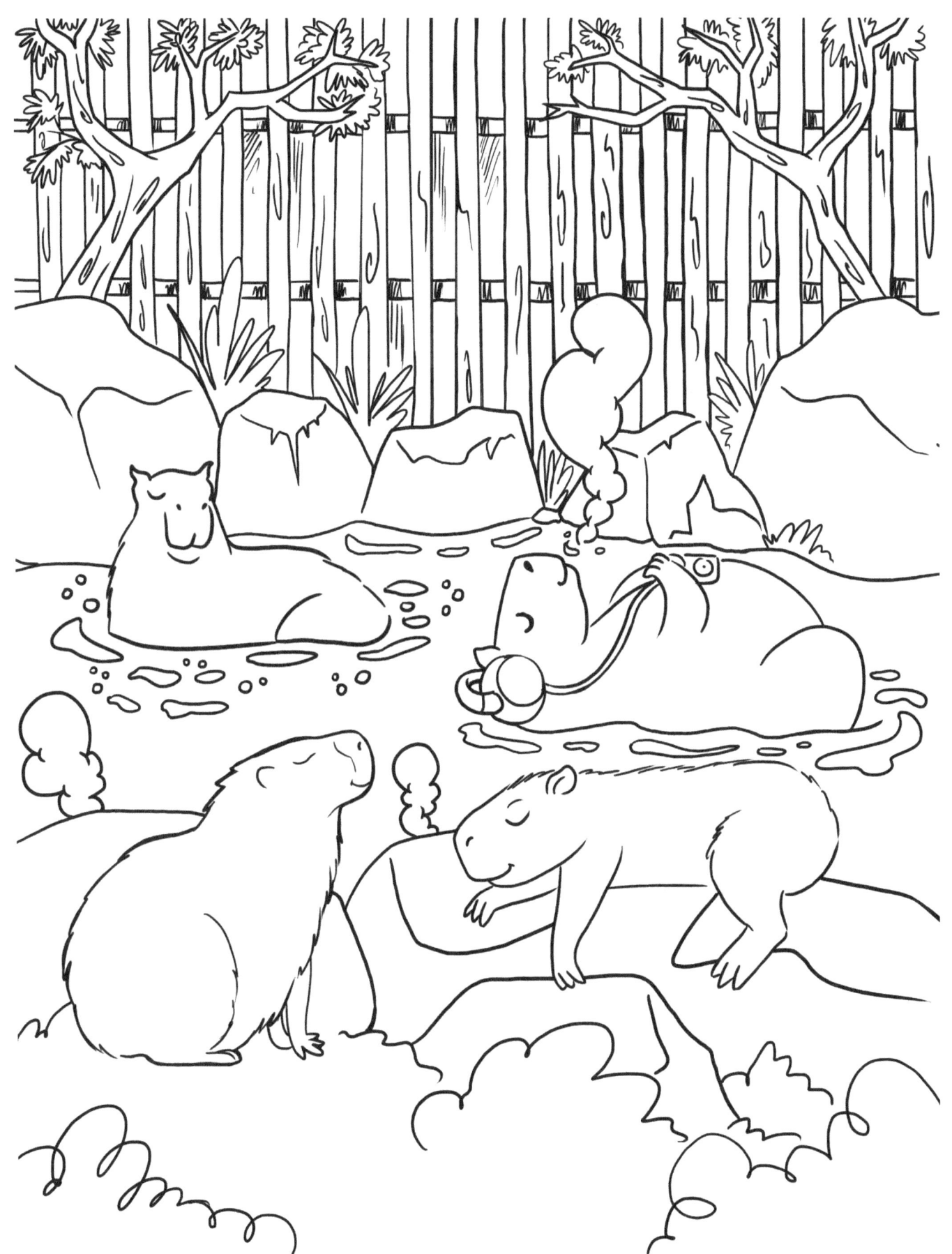

Swim, swim, swim all day! Check out those slightly webbed toes.

Capybara feet are designed for aqua adventures.

Oh, and those ears can be pressed against the head to keep water out. No swim cap needed here!

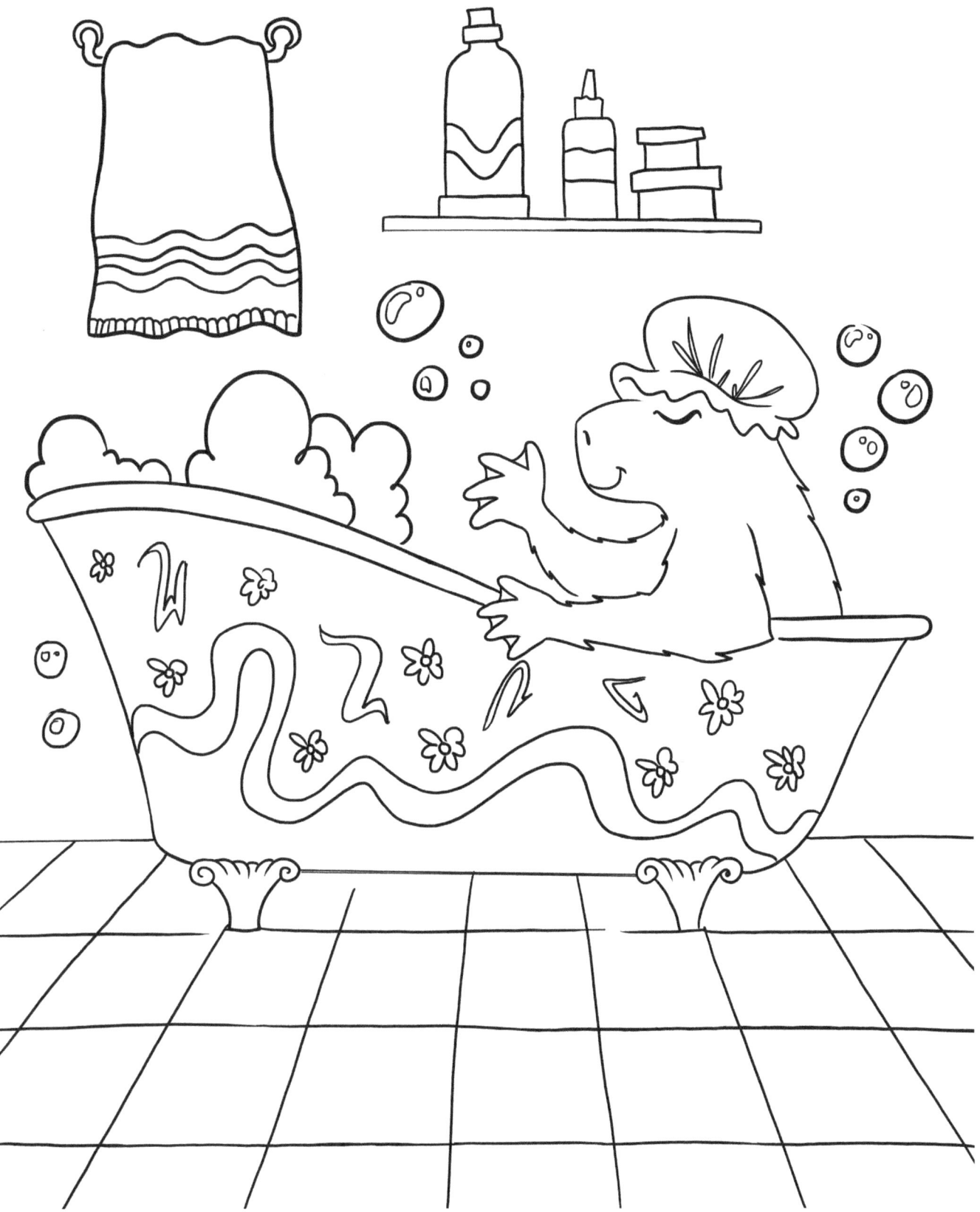

Capybaras can stay underwater for up to 5 minutes.

Kids, don't try this at home.

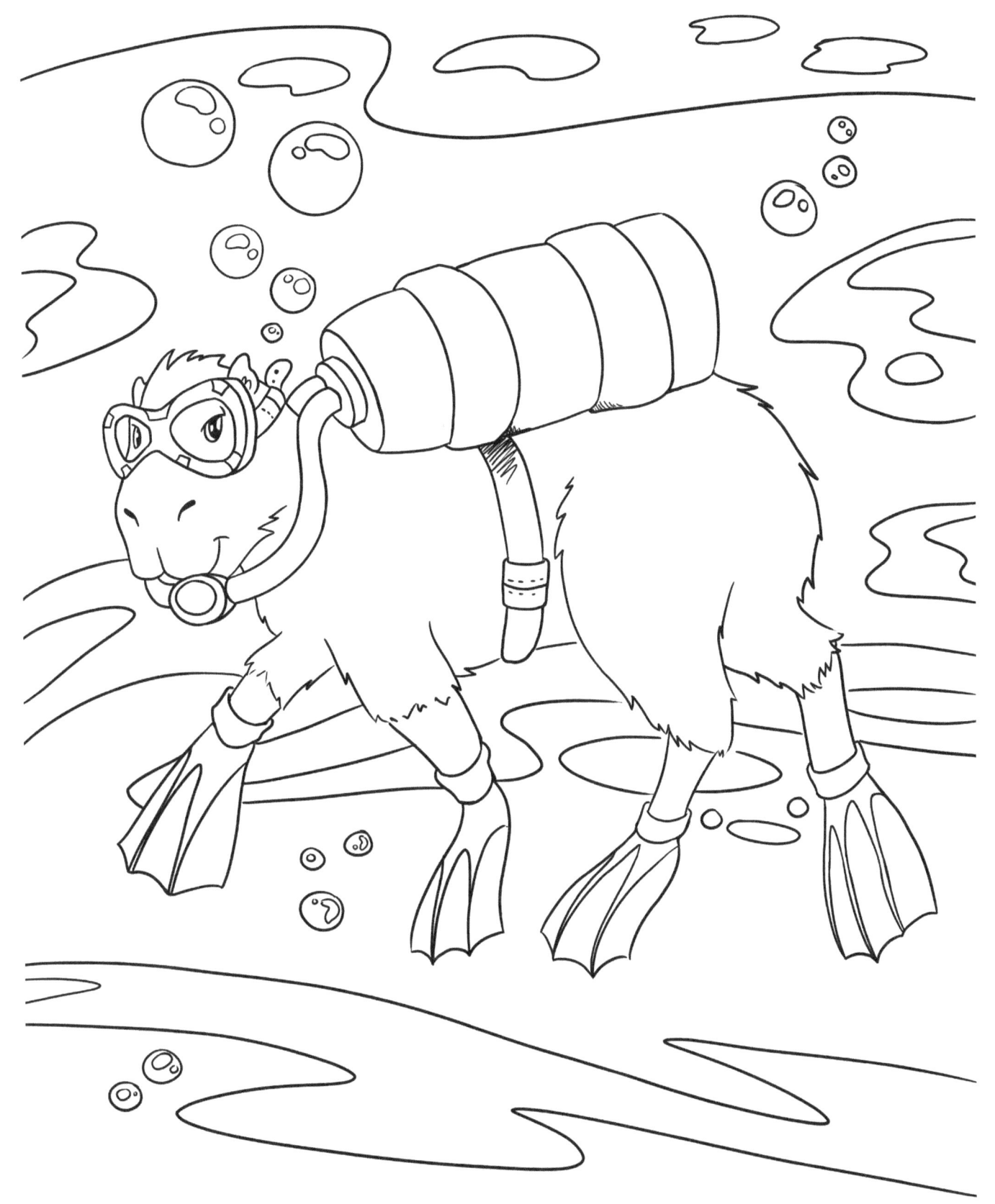

What do jaguars, eagles, caimans, anacondas, and humans have in common?

They are all *predators* of our humble capybara.

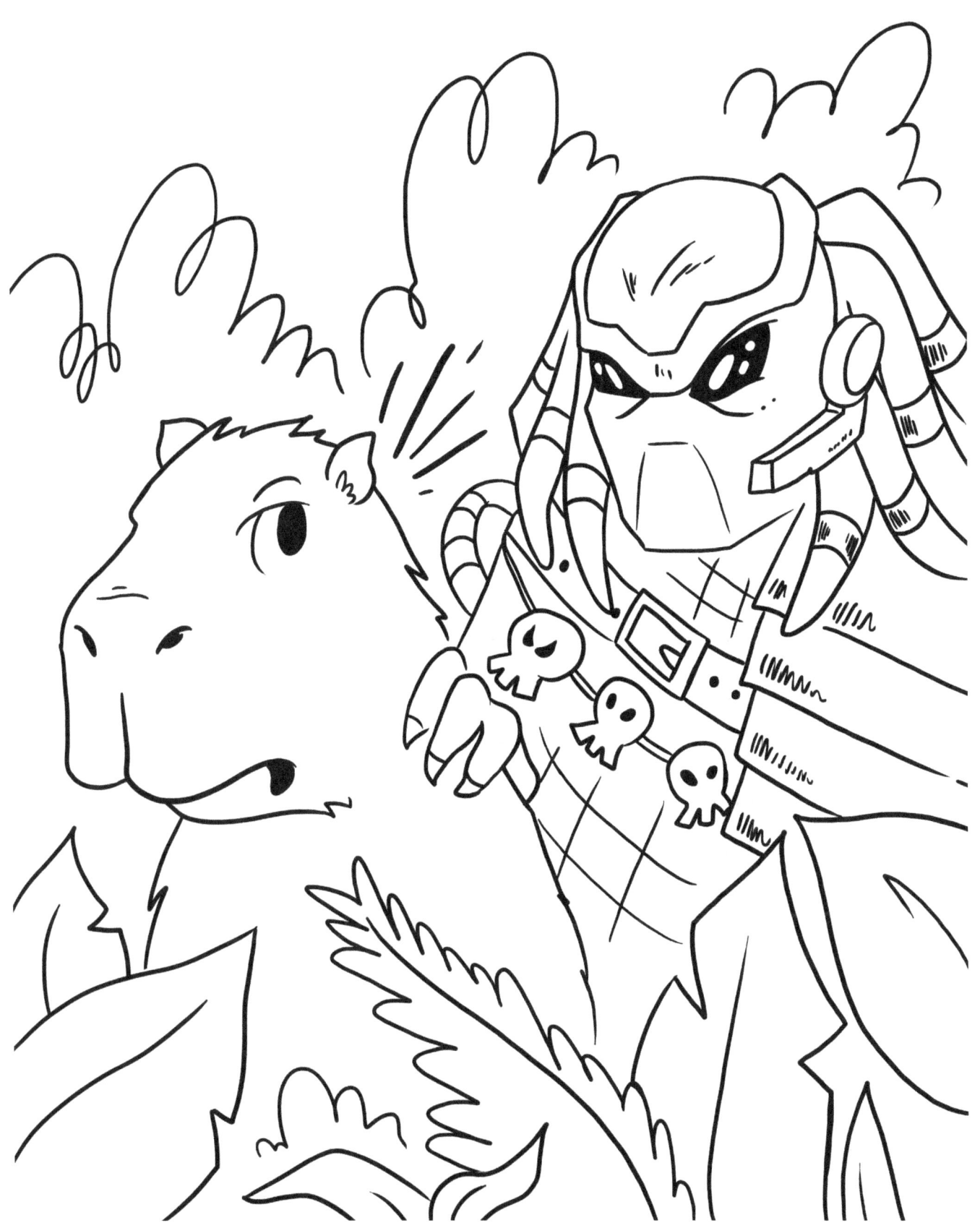

What's really cute, drinks water, eats grass, and sometimes eats its own poop and vomit? If you said a capybara (a good guess for all questions in this book…), *you are correct*!

Like larger land mammals and ruminants, capybaras sometimes re-digest their most recent meal to absorb more nutrients. It adds nice variety to their otherwise grass and veggie diet. Yum!!

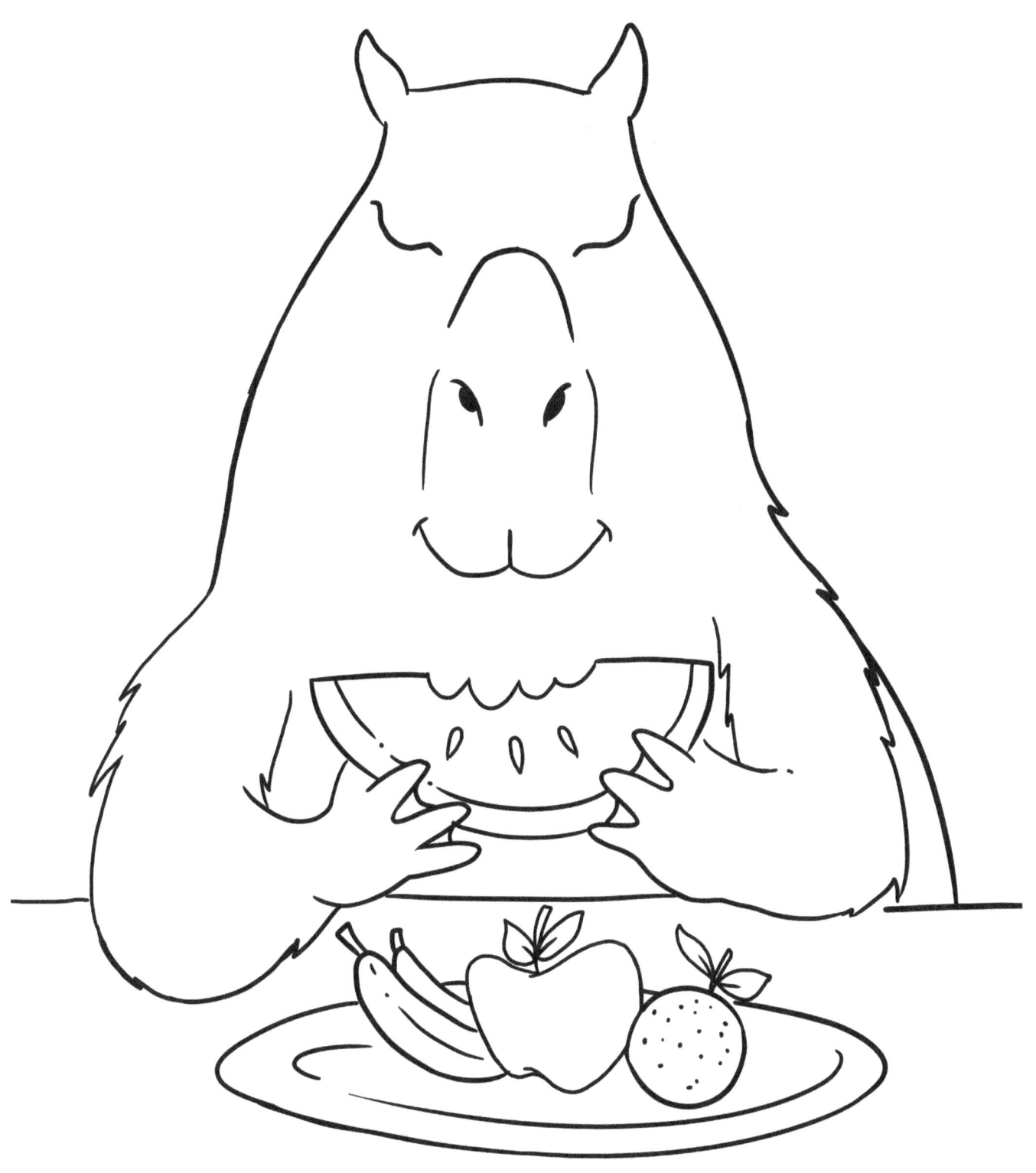

Capybaras seem to bring out the best of puns.

Guinea bigs.

Don't worry, be capy.

Capy birthday to you!

Capy-tivating coloring book, don't you think?

What's your favorite capybara pun or joke?

_____

_____

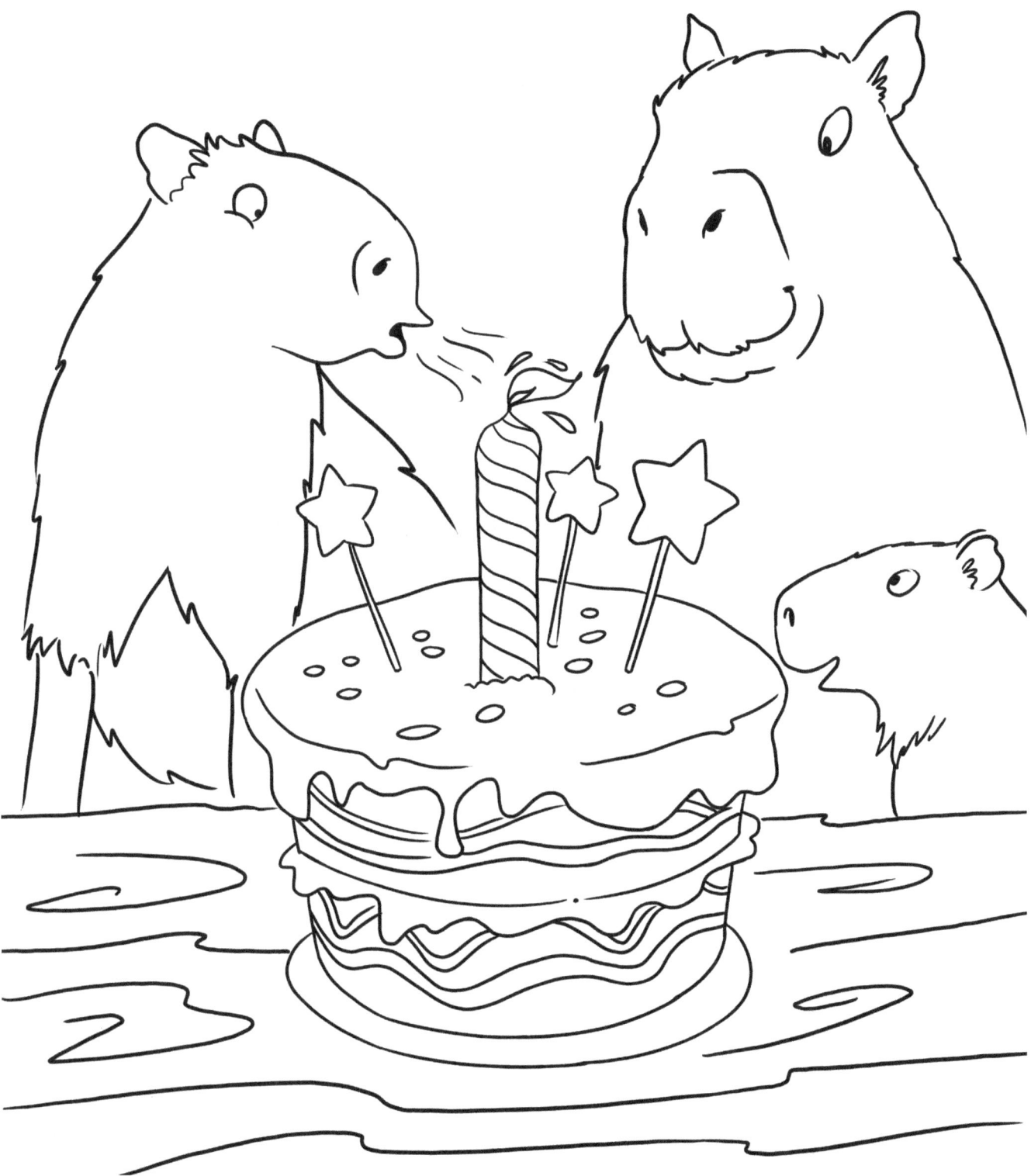

Like other rodents, capybaras are known for their intelligence (in addition to their good looks!).

While some have been used as guide animals, we don't yet have examples of the capybara being used to assist police investigations.

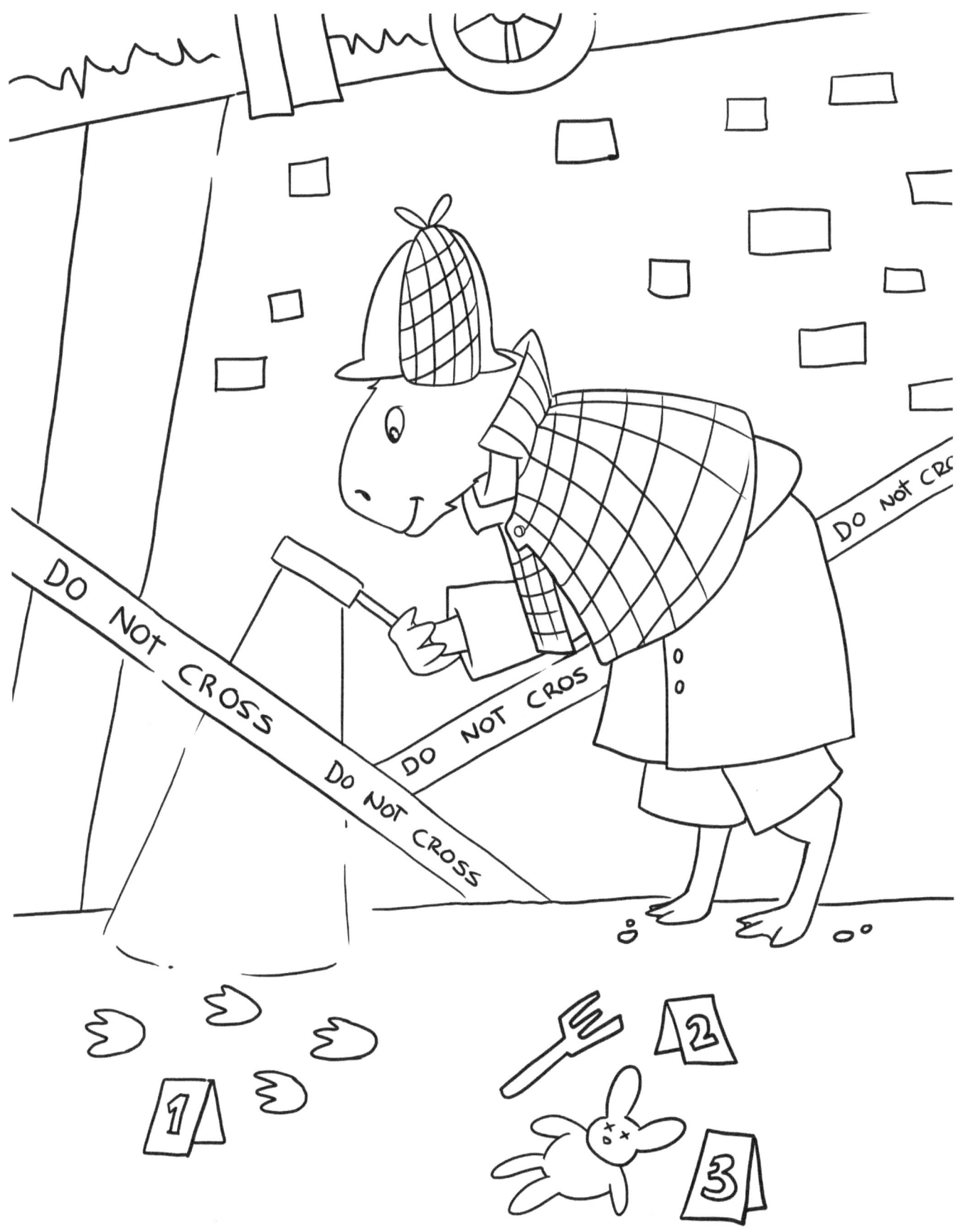

Next time you're looking for an alternate milk to go with your coffee, ask your barista for capybara milk!

Baby capybaras start grazing on grasses after just a few days, but they will supplement with mamma capybara's milk for about 16 weeks.

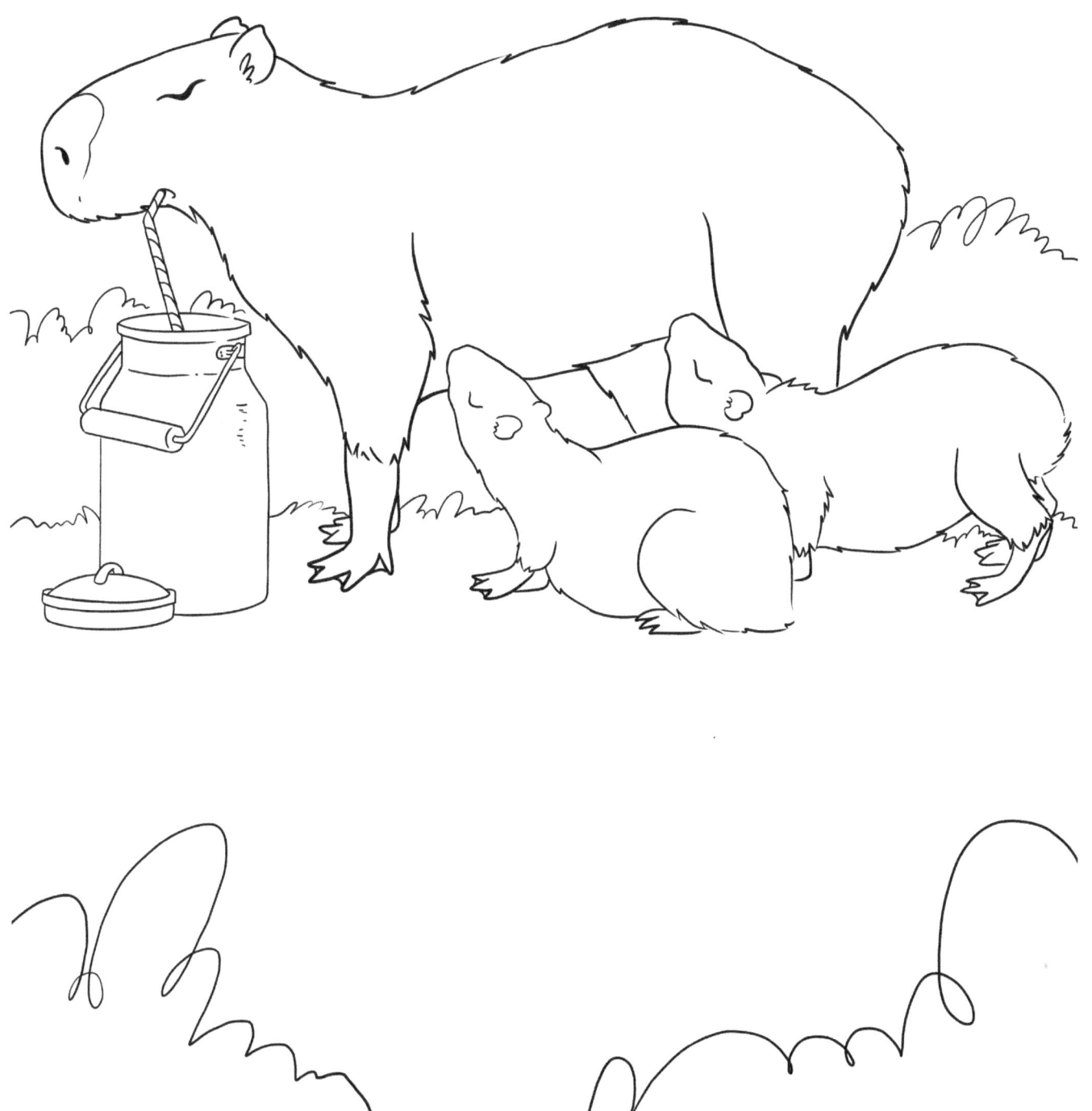

If you ever get to time travel, make sure to make a stop in the 16th Century.

This is when the Catholic Church classified the capybara as a fish because of all the time it spent in the water.

This practice has remained 5 centuries later; capybara meat is popular during Lent and the Holy Week, because, well, it's "fish", not meat!

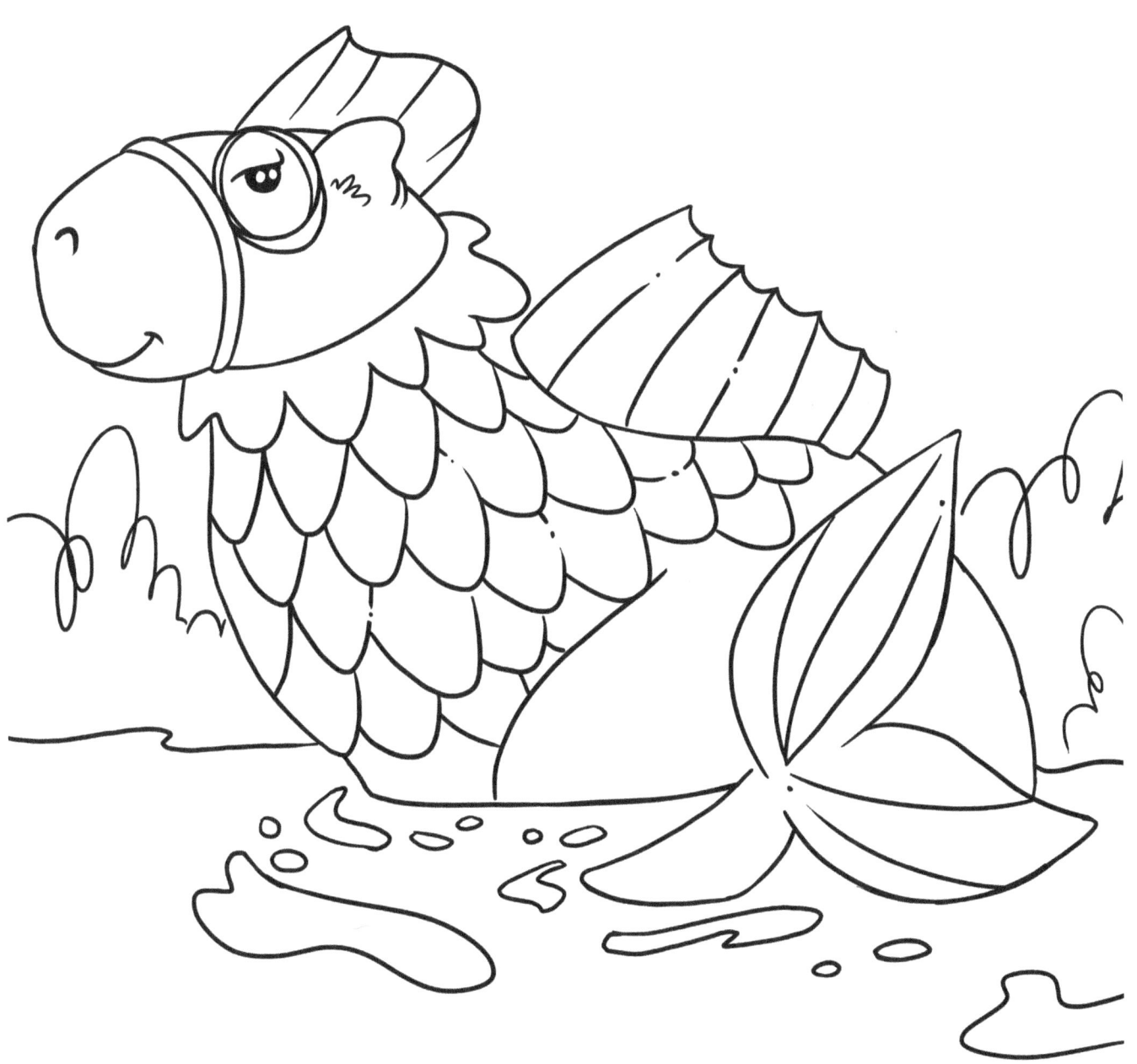

In case you are a fan of radioactive turtles trained in the way of the Ninja, you should know that they were trained by a rat…not a capybara.

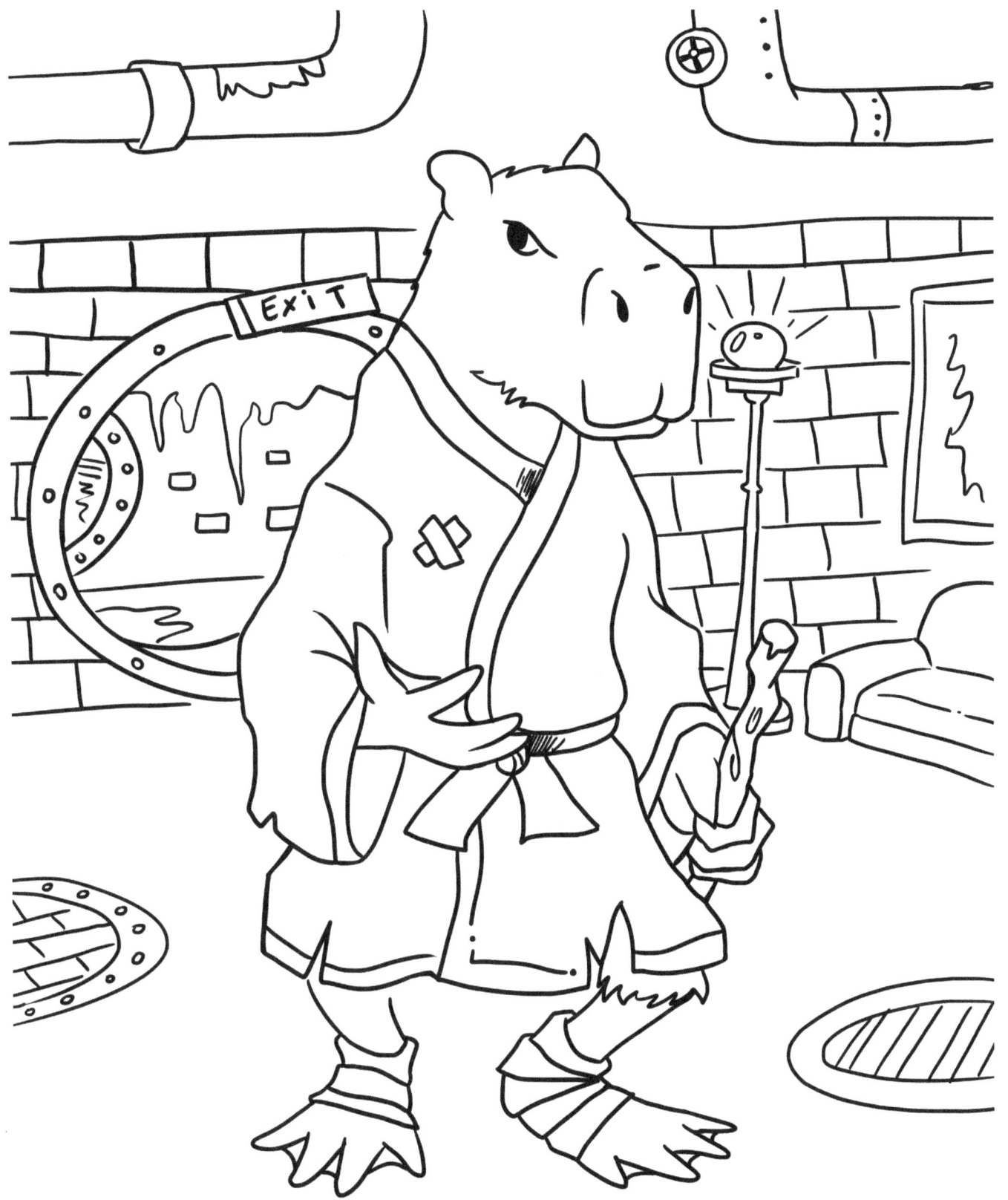

Capybara farm...that sounds awesome!

Not so fast.

Capybaras are farmed for their meat and leather.

We hope the capybaras reading this book will learn from this and hide better.

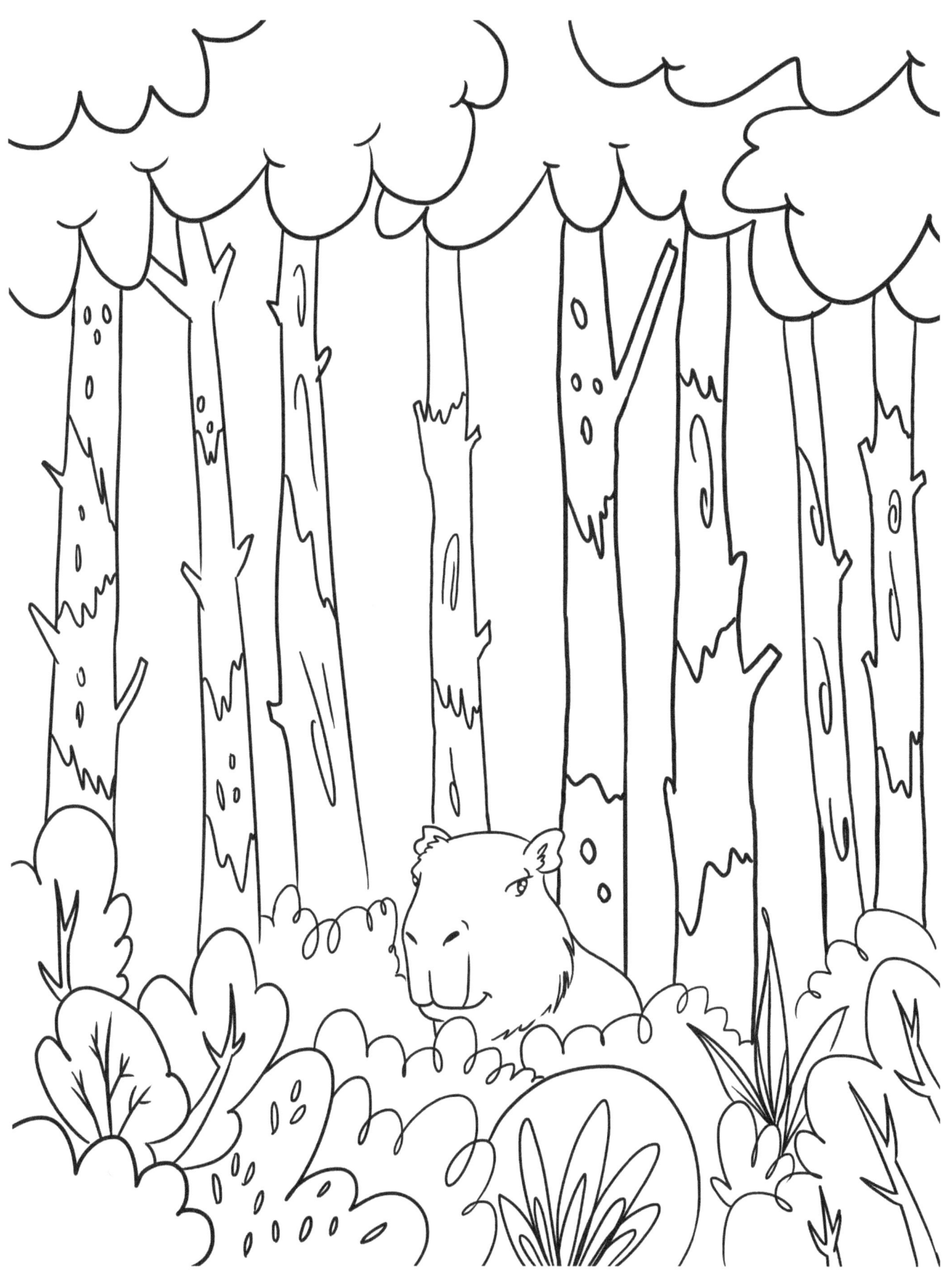

Capybaras often live in groups of about 10.

This gives the groups a chance to decide which capybaras will specialize in what skills like farmer, hairdresser, tactical defense, building the website, architecture, and robotics.

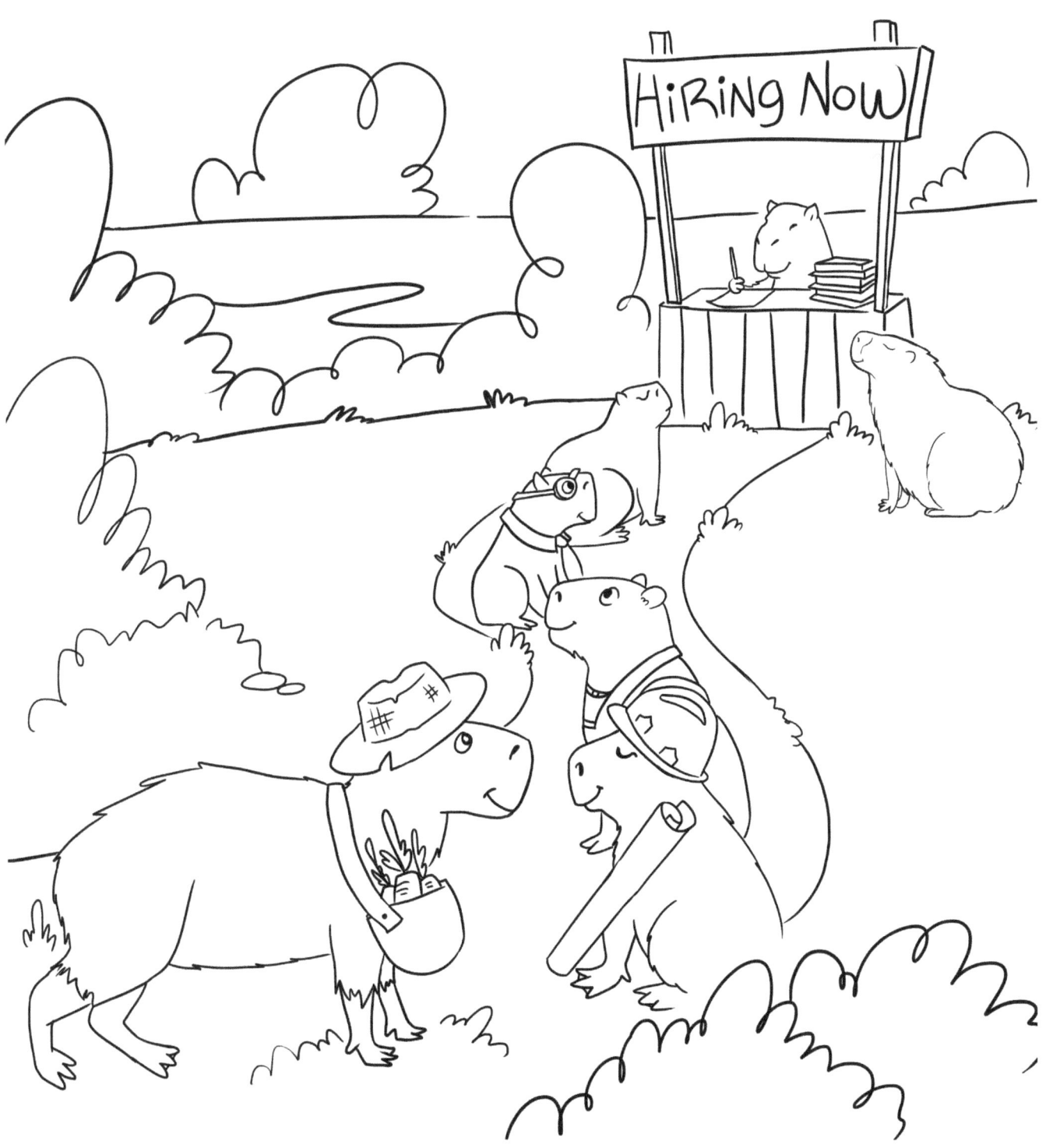

Let's color this one by letter!

R = Red
O = Orange
Y = Yellow
G = Green
Bl = Blue
V = Violet
B = Brown

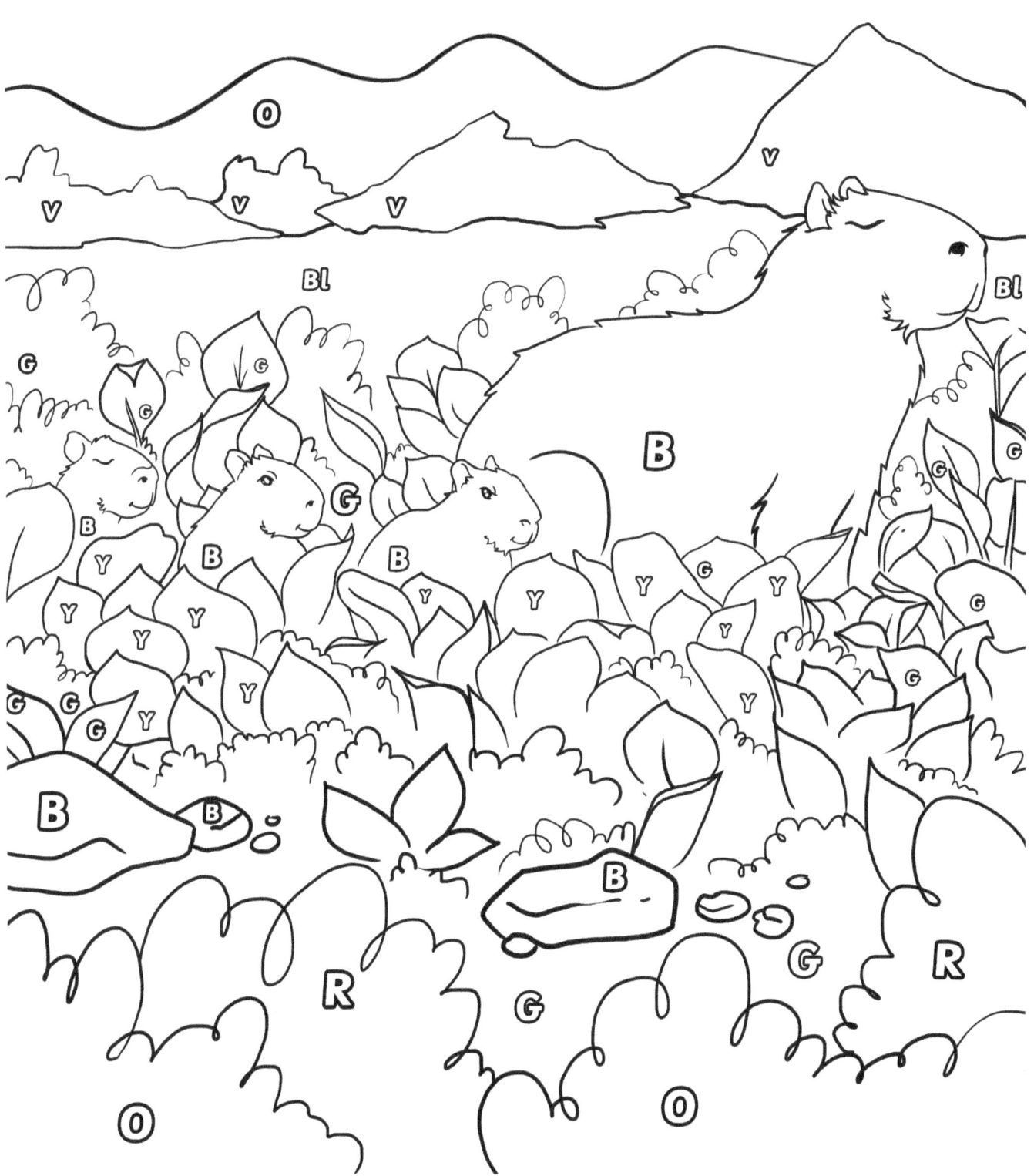

Everyone likes to sit on the capybara!

Birds...

Primates...

Turtles...

Other capybaras ...

I, however, think these guinea *bigs* are way too cute to be used as chairs.

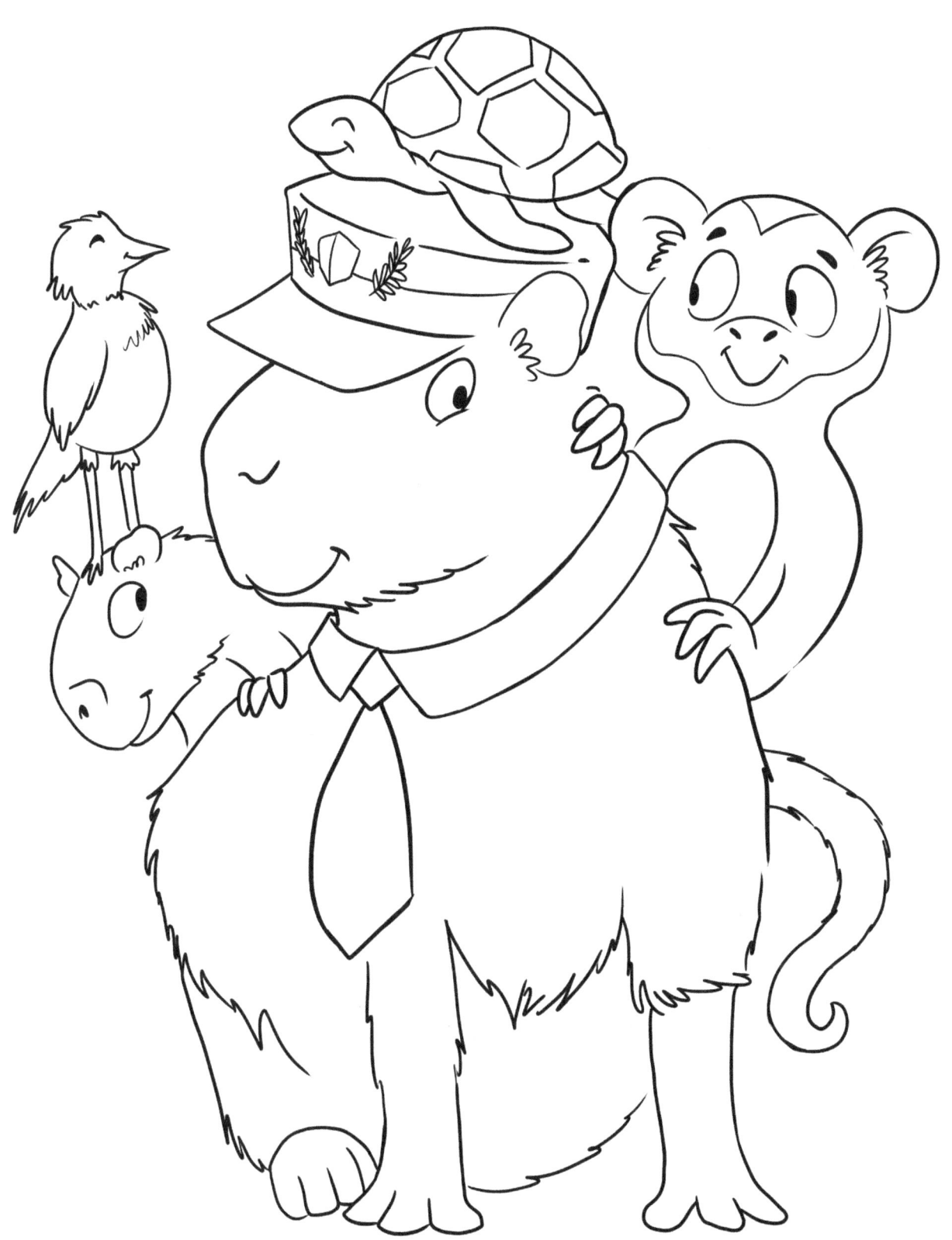

Watch your finger! Those teeth are super sharp!! This isn't just to impress the dentist.

Capybara teeth grow throughout the rodent's lifetime to allow them to slice right through the tough grasses in their diet. Normal grass consumption files down the teeth and keeps them at acceptable, toothy lengths.

Q: What's a capybara's favorite time to go the dentist?

A: Tooth-hurty! (2:30)

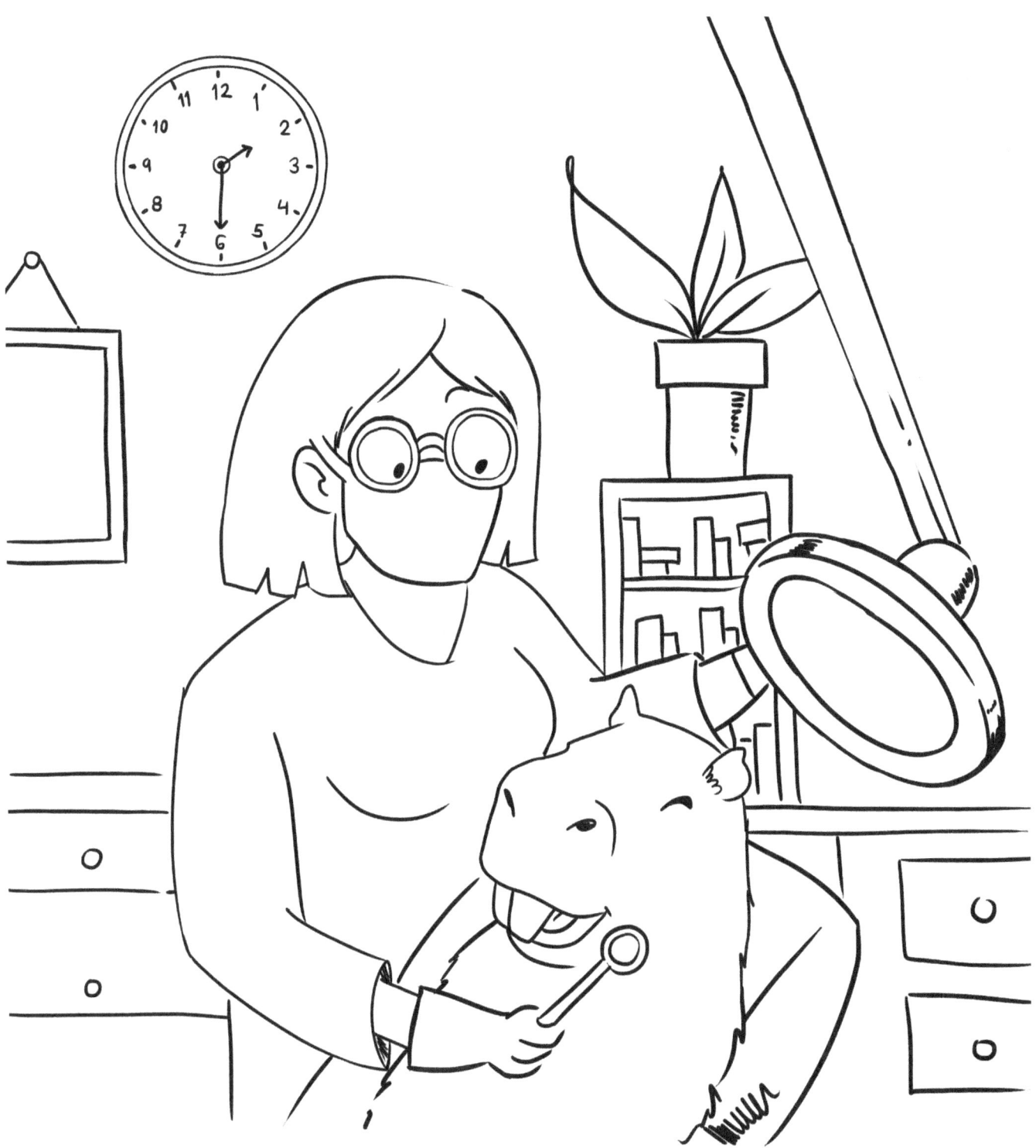

If you've ever seen a capybara dating show or soap opera, you'll be familiar with the super entertaining whistling noises female capybaras make to attract nearby males.

The best part: the whistle noise is made with her nose! Talk about a nosy noise!

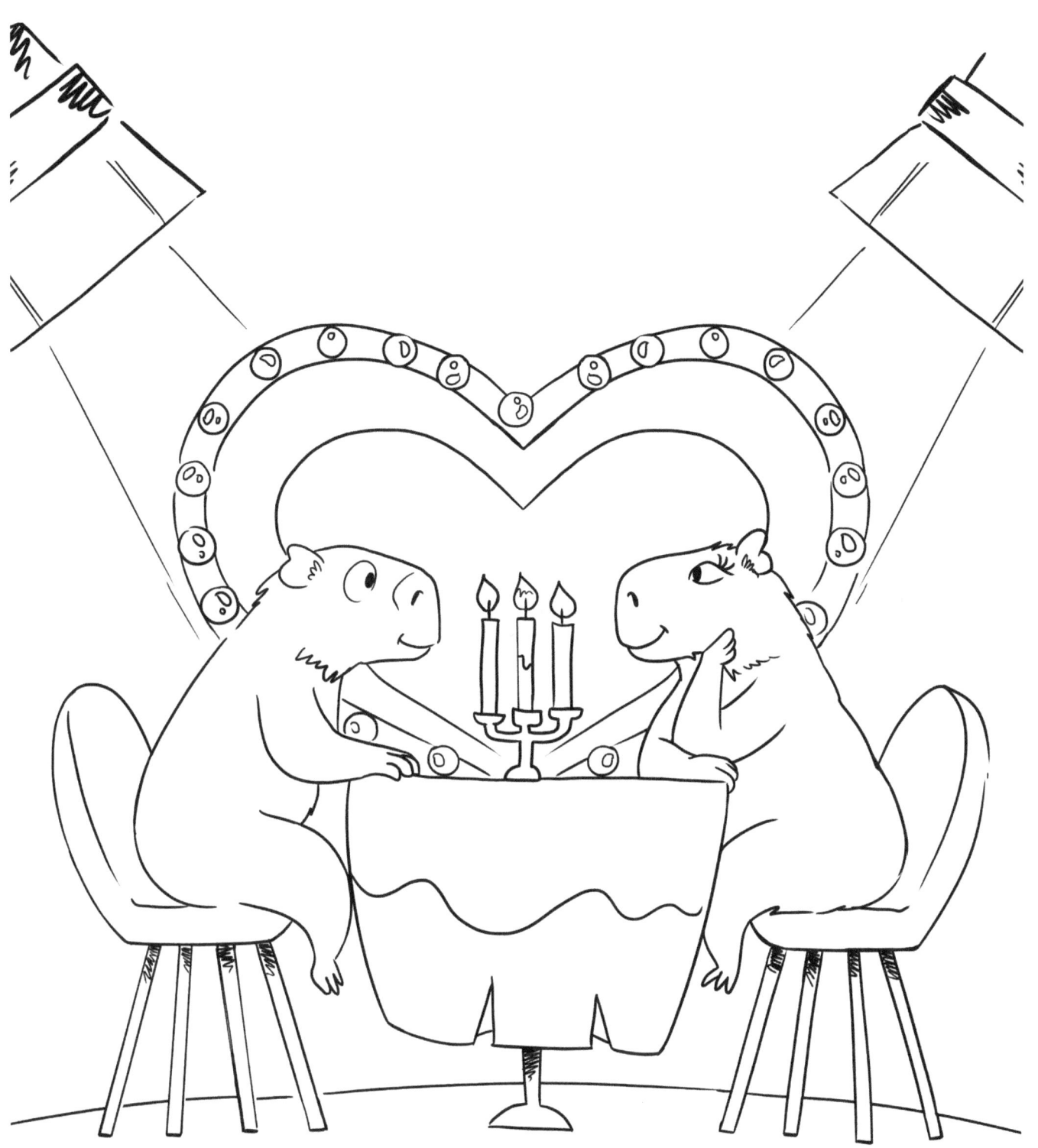

While the answer to the Ultimate Question of Life may be 42 in some circles, most capybaras arrive to Earth in litters of 4.

Litter size may range from 1-8 pups.

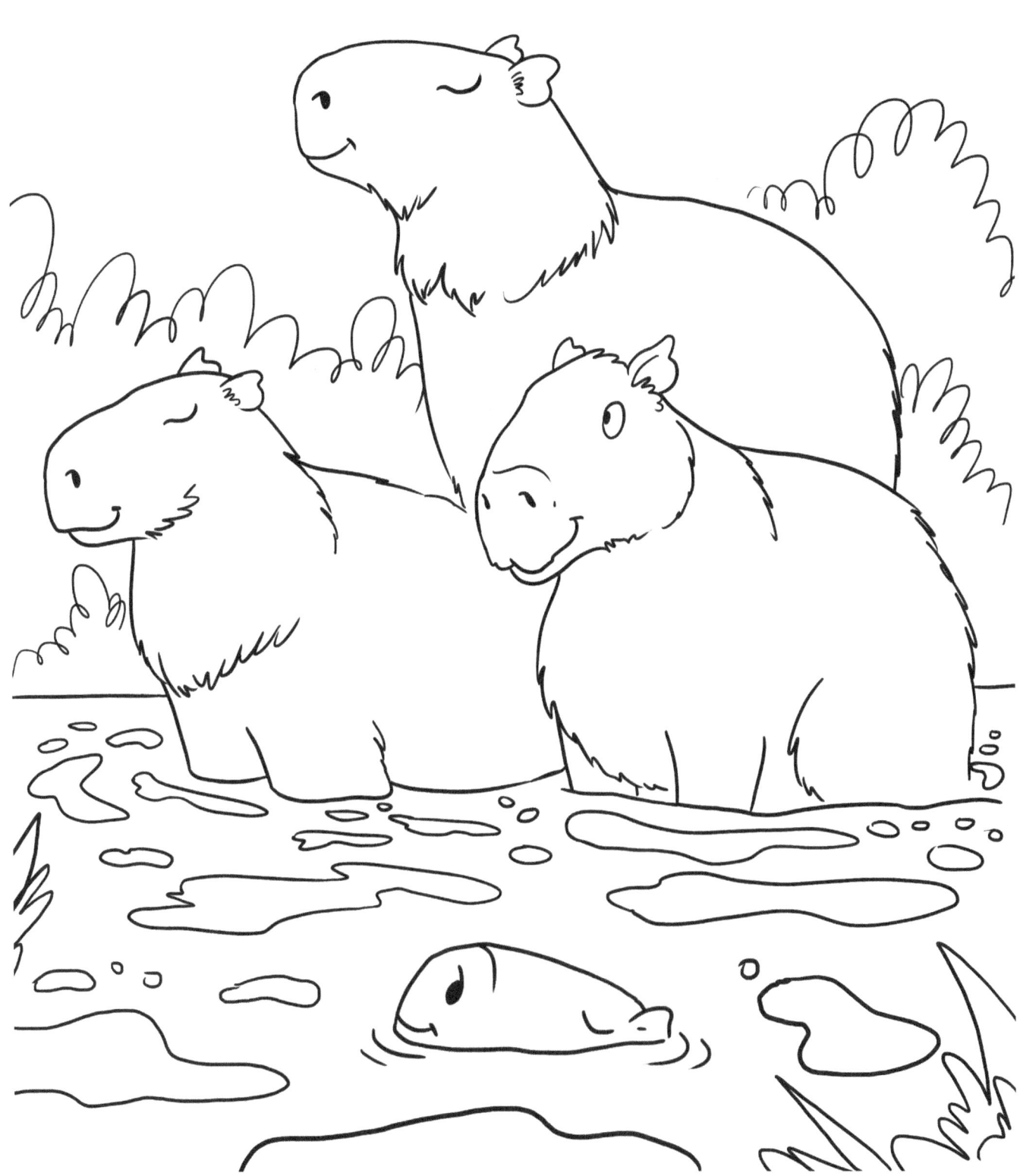

While capybaras are aquatic animals, the pups are born on the land.

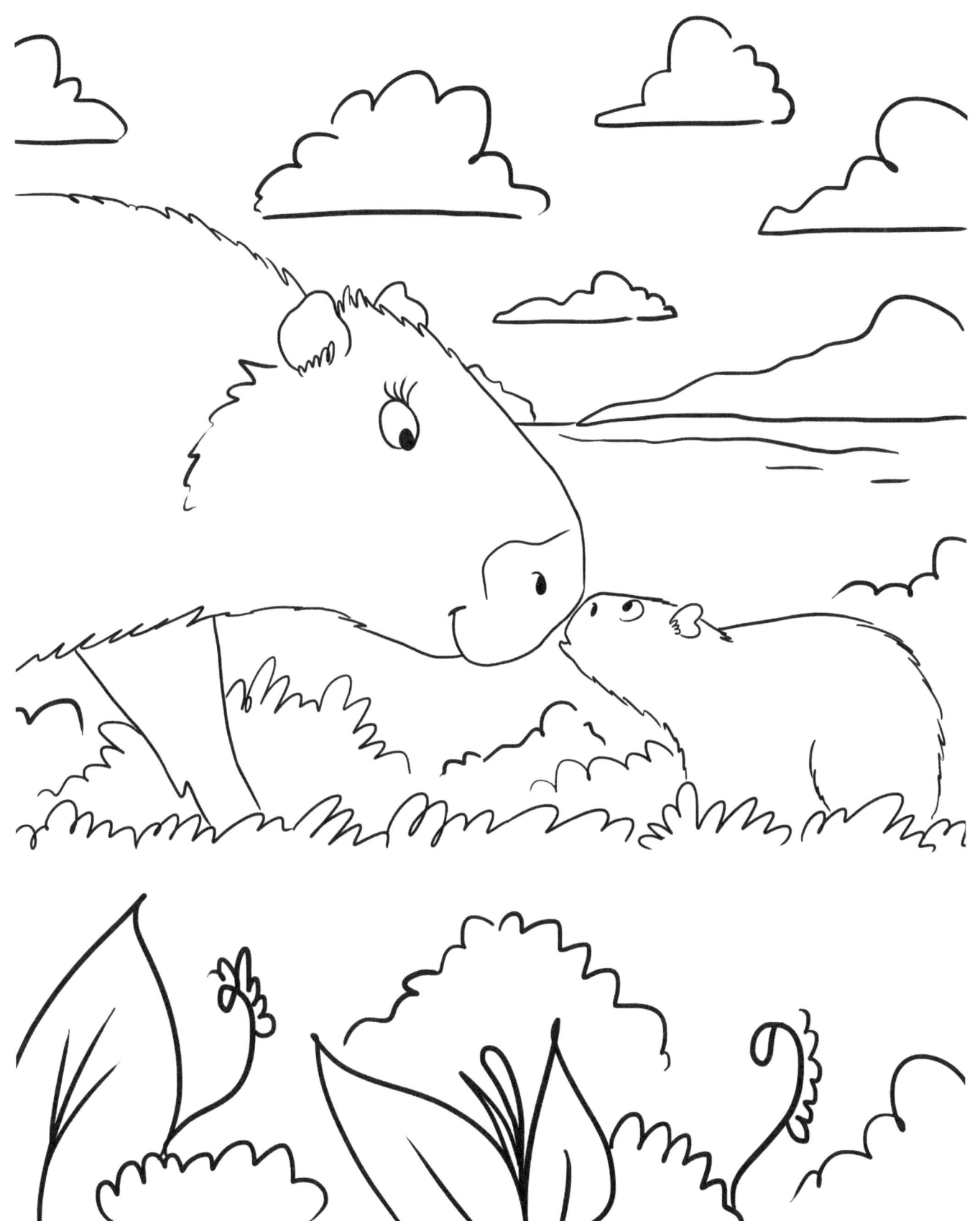

Some of our favorite superhero comics have capybara stars.

What's the name of your favorite capybara superhero?

_____

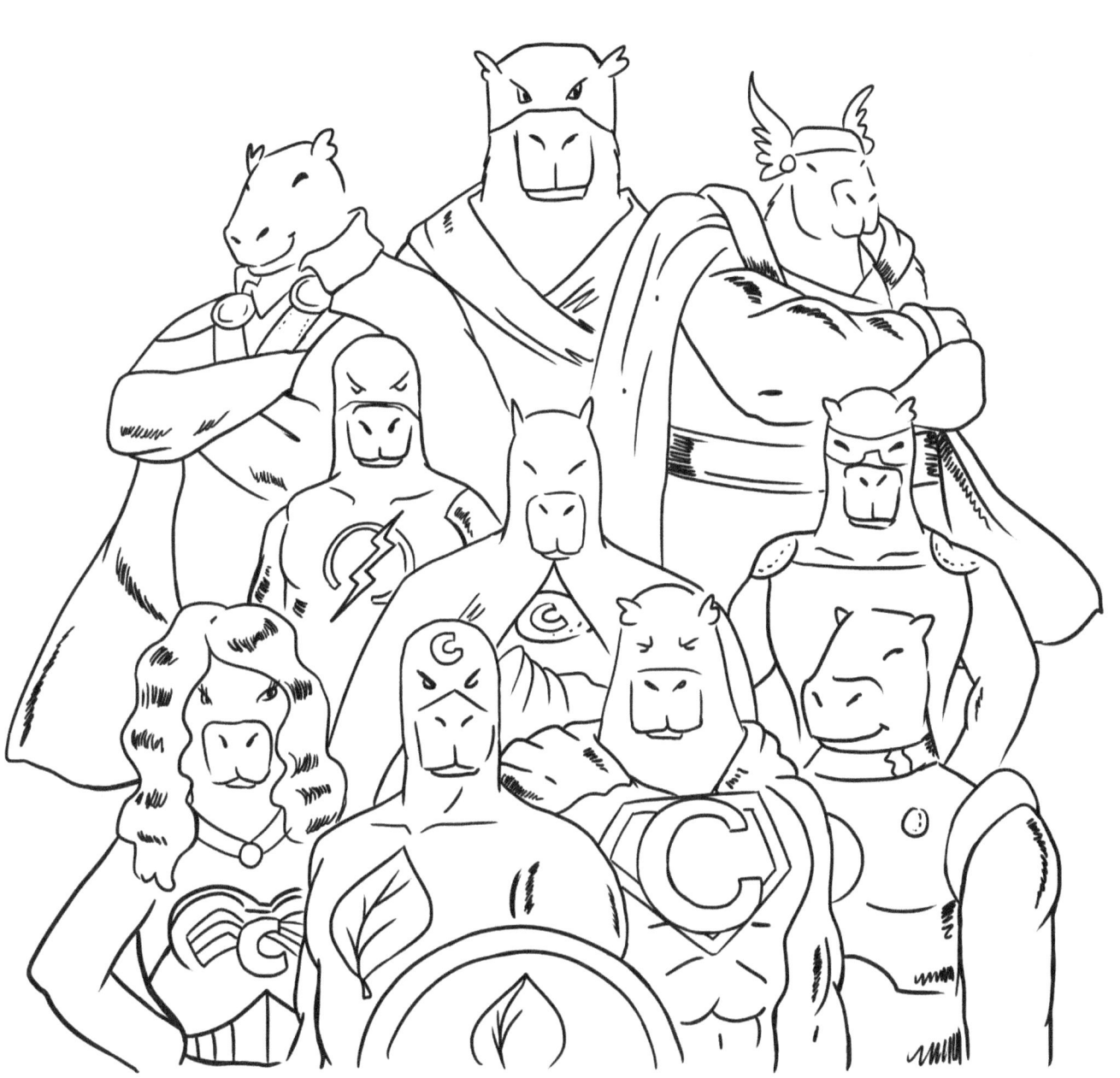

Time for a CAP-LIB!

The _____ (animal, singular noun) is the world's BIGGEST rodent found in most of _____ (magical place).

These animals really like to eat _____ (plural noun), _____ (plural noun), and _____ (adjective) _____ (plural noun).

They are known for their _____ (body part, plural), which can be razor-sharp. In fact, some describe them as _____ (adjective) _____ (noun) because of their _____ (adjective) _____ (plural noun).

These animals sometimes _____ (verb) in rivers and streams. When this happens, they _____ (verb) with _____ (animal, plural noun) and make an odor that smells like _____ (adjective) _____ (noun).

If I met a/an _____ (animal, same as first answer above) in the wild, I would name it _____ (color) - _____ (adjective) _____ (last thing you ate), and we would color together!

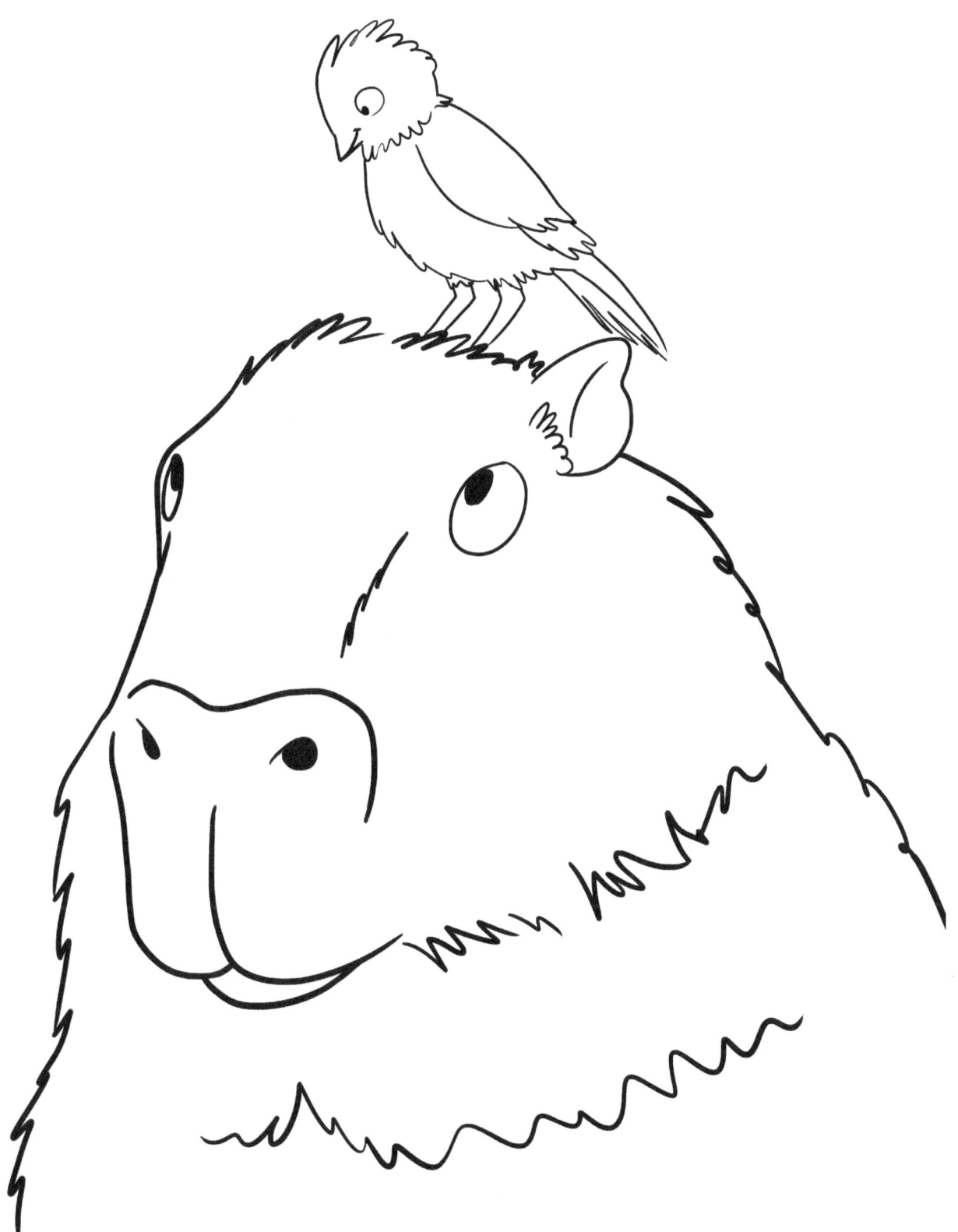

***Zzzzzzzzzzz* {snore}** *zzzzzzzzzzzzz*

Capybaras sometimes *zzzzzzz* fall asleep in the water, with only their noses up above the water line.

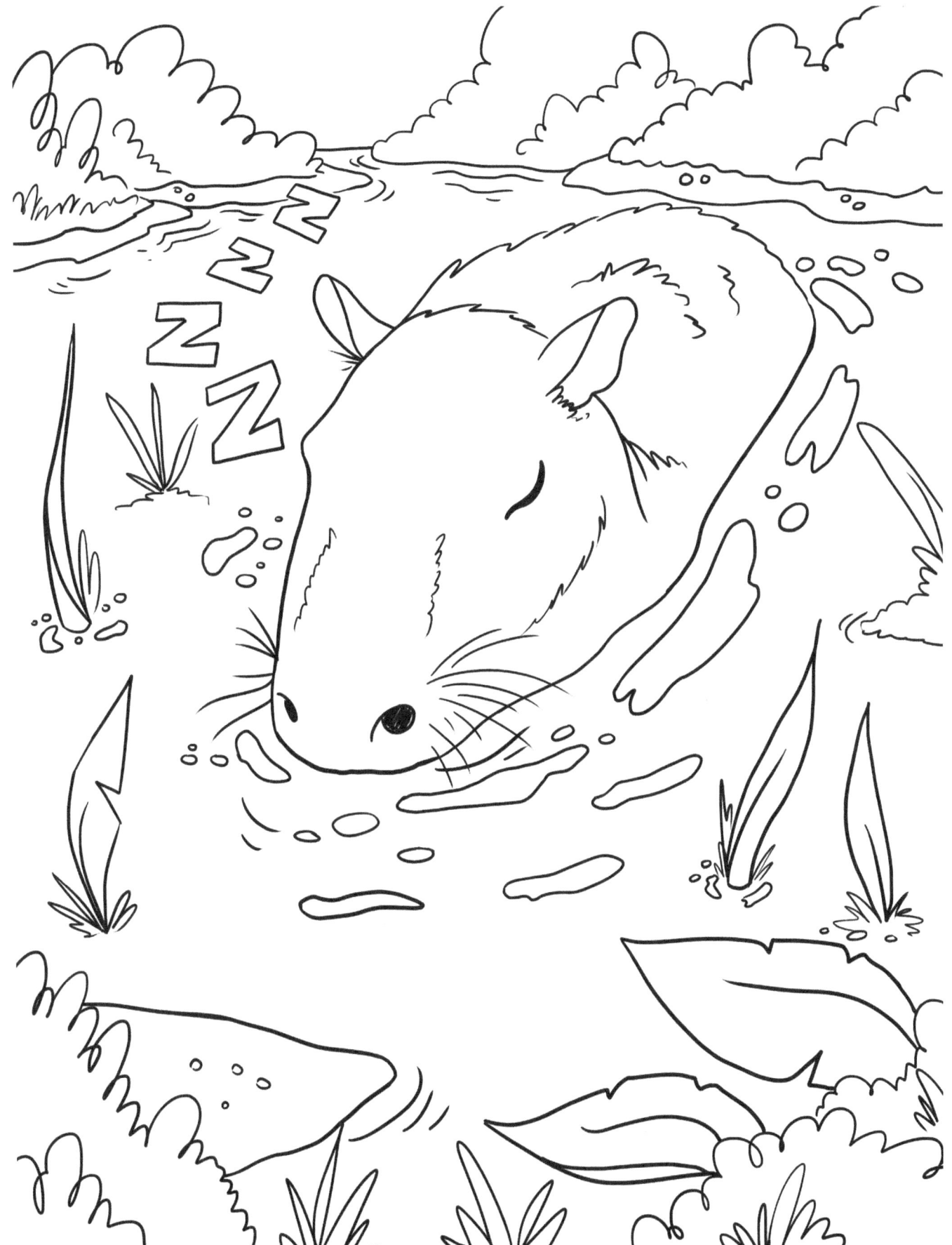

Fortunately, capybaras are not considered endangered.

Their population is relatively stable, though hunting and habitat destruction have reduced their overall population.

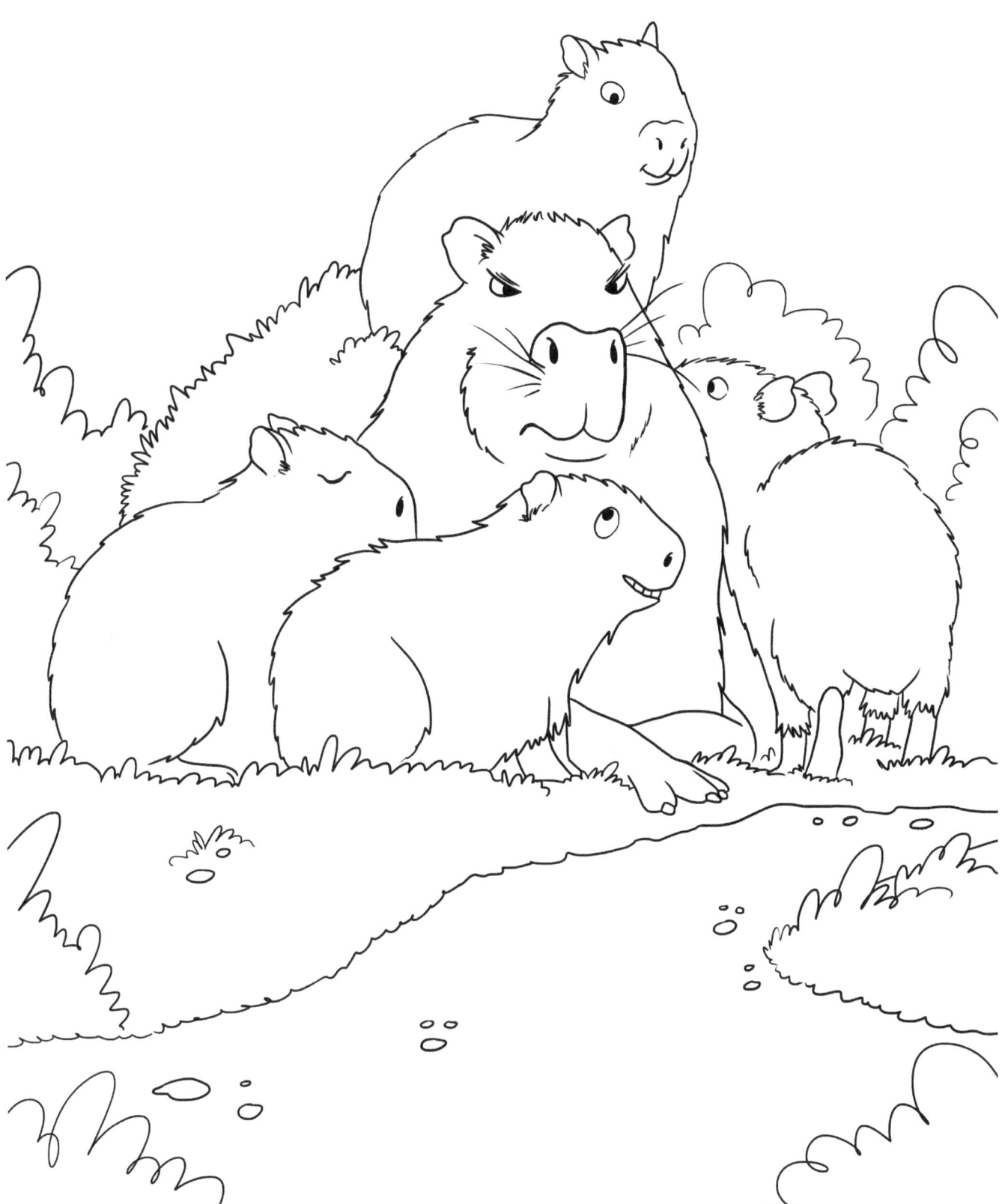

Some capybaras live in the city!

While some ride in limousines, most prefer to go by bus, taxi, bicycle, or skateboard because they want to take good care of the environment.

Obviously.

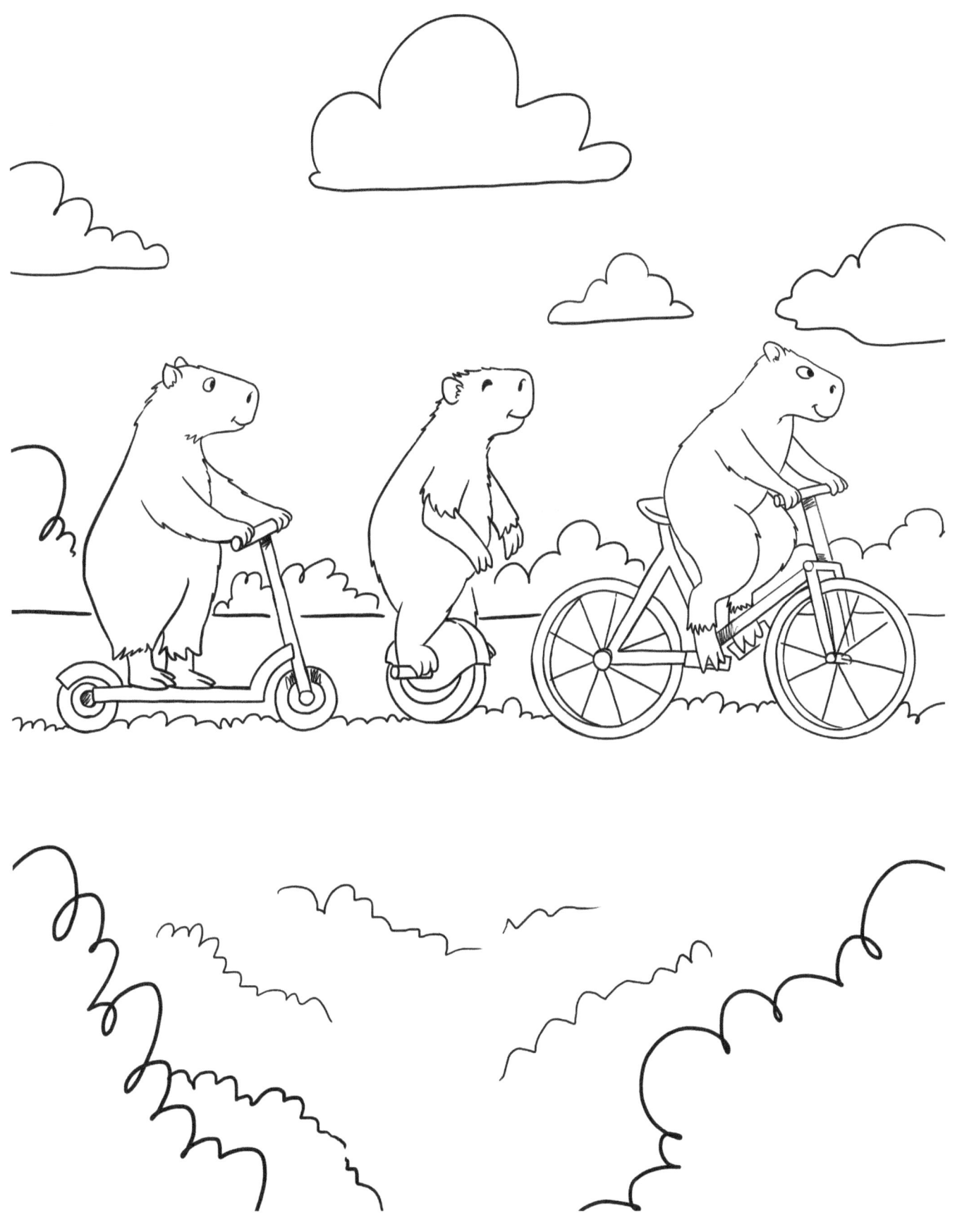

Capybaras, unlike vampires, are not immortal, nor are they sensitive to garlic or light.

Most capybaras live for about 4 years in the wild, though they can live up to 12 years in captivity.

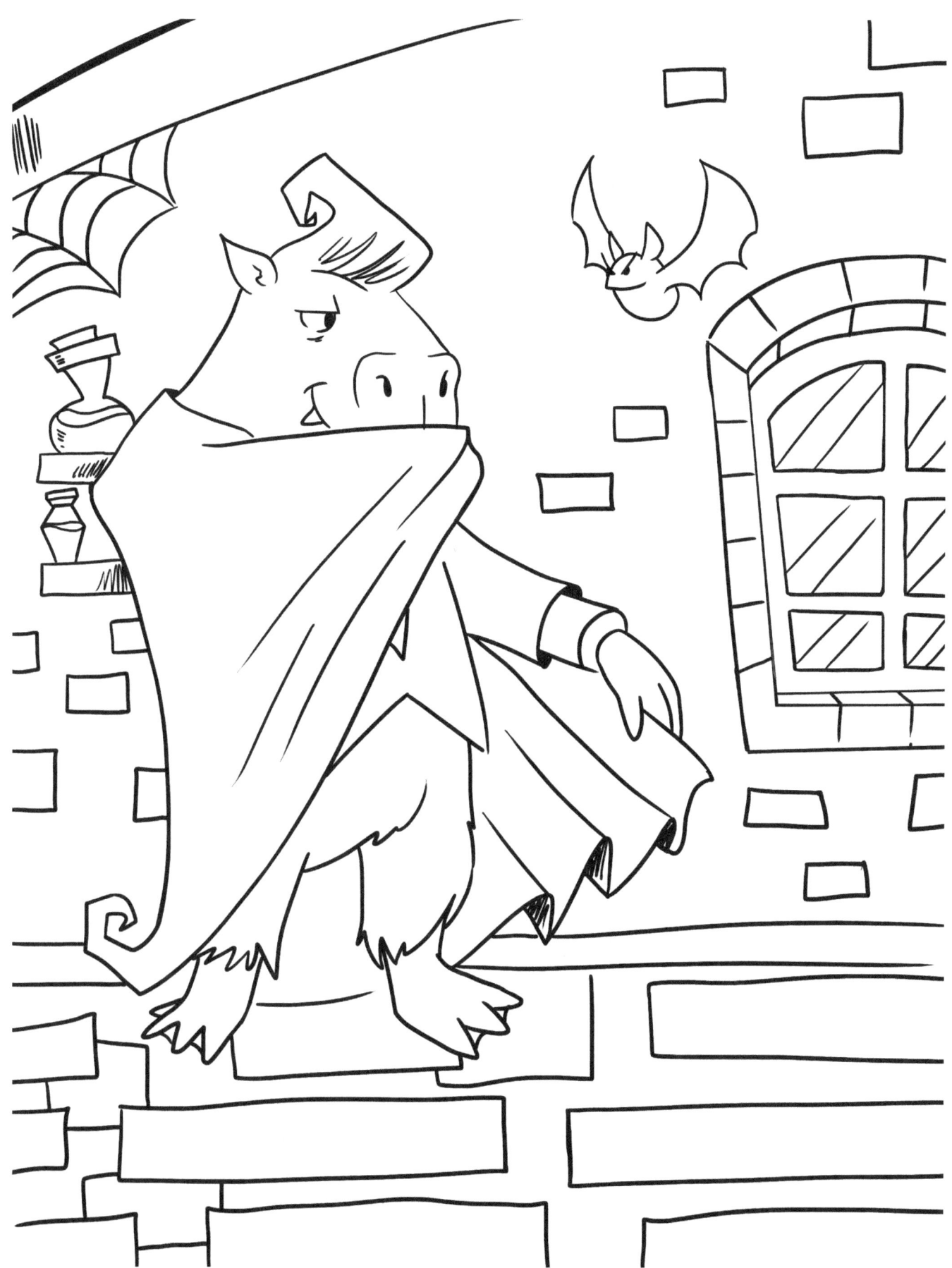

How about another color-by-letter?

We decided not to label this one, so you could create a totally random image!

To color this one, randomly (*without looking at our guide below*) write the letters A – G in empty spots in the image on the next place. Then, color the image using this guide:

- a) Red
- b) Orange
- c) Yellow
- d) Green
- e) Blue
- f) Violet
- g) Brown

Make sure to send us your cool colorings to share!

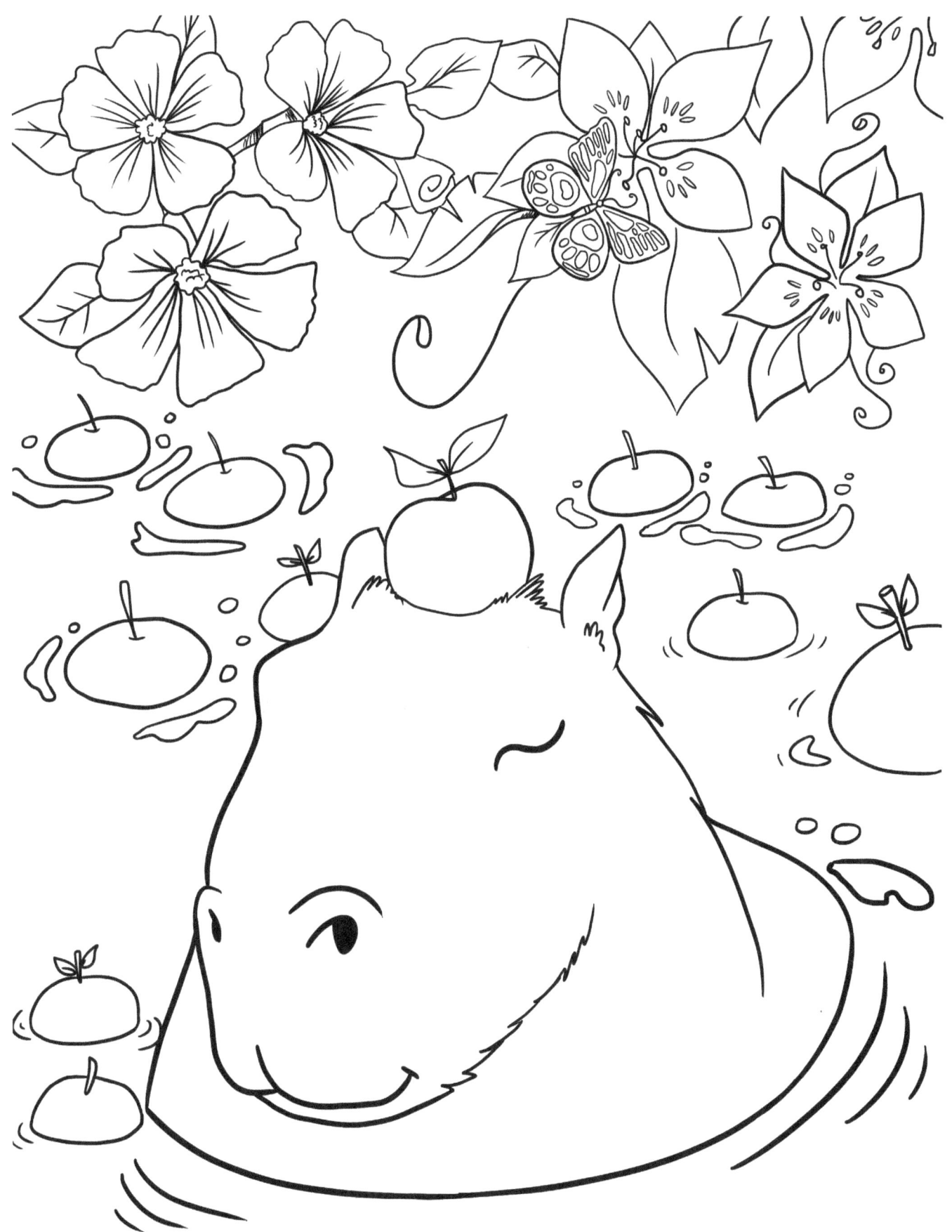

In boxing and martial arts, contestants are separated into categories of weight.

So, you should probably know that the heaviest female capybara ever weighed in Brazil was 91kg (201 pounds)!

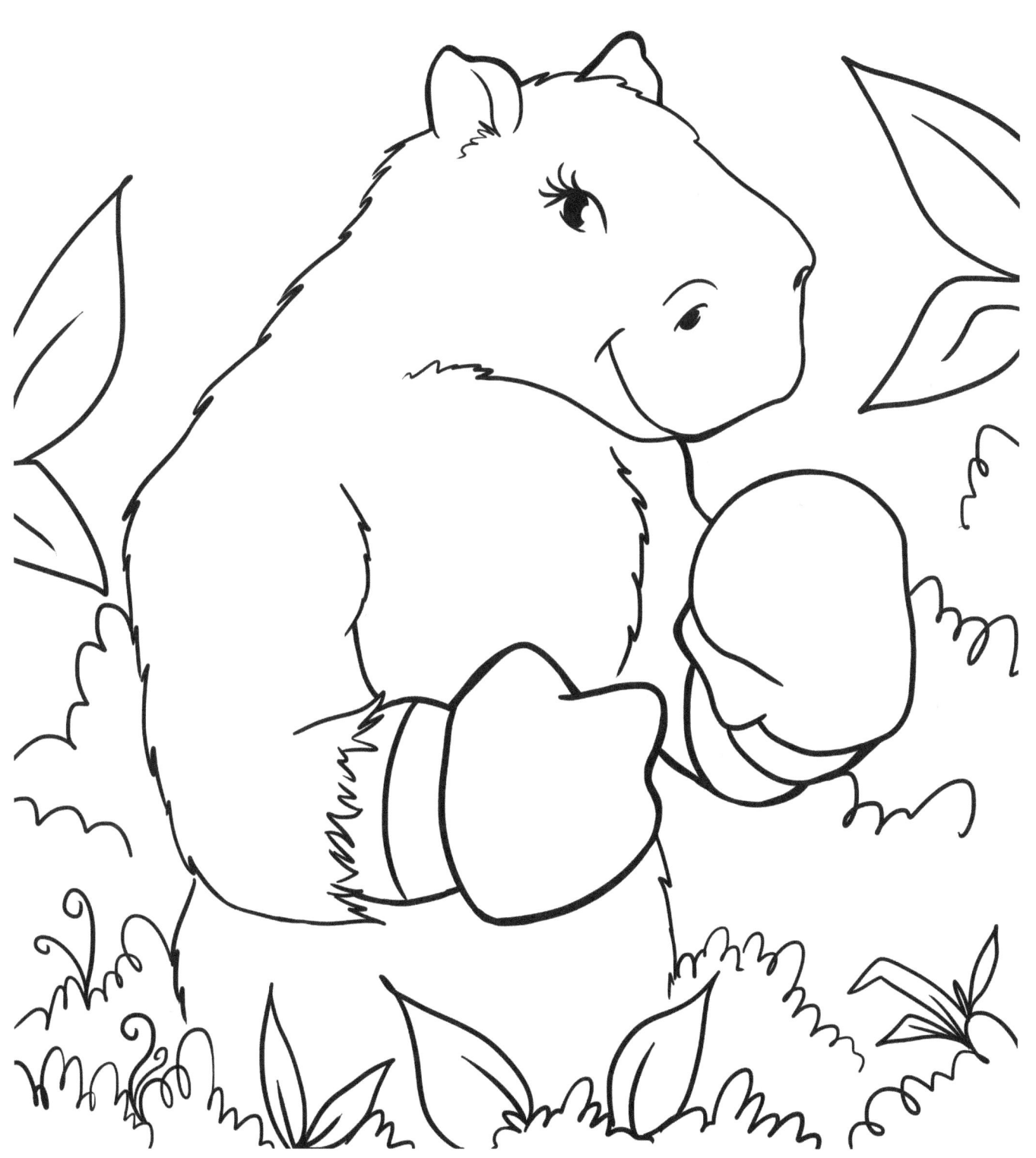

What's that smell? If you said a sweaty capybara -- which is a safe bet in most situations -- you are correct!

Capybaras have sweat glands in their fur to help keep them extra *capy-tivating*.

This adds to their mystique and allure.

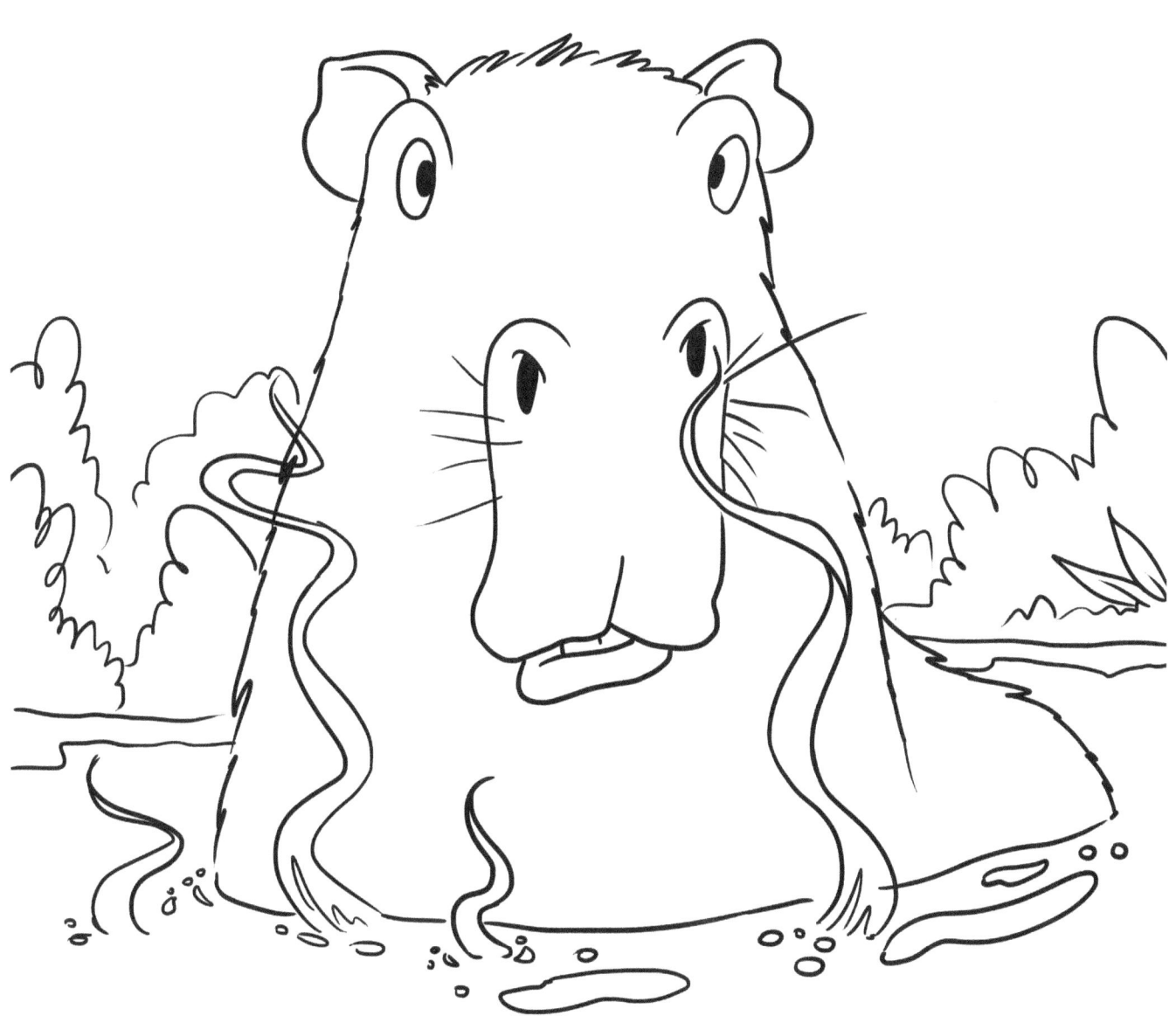

INSTANT DANCE PARTY. Can you dance like a capybara?

CAPY CAPY

JOY JOY

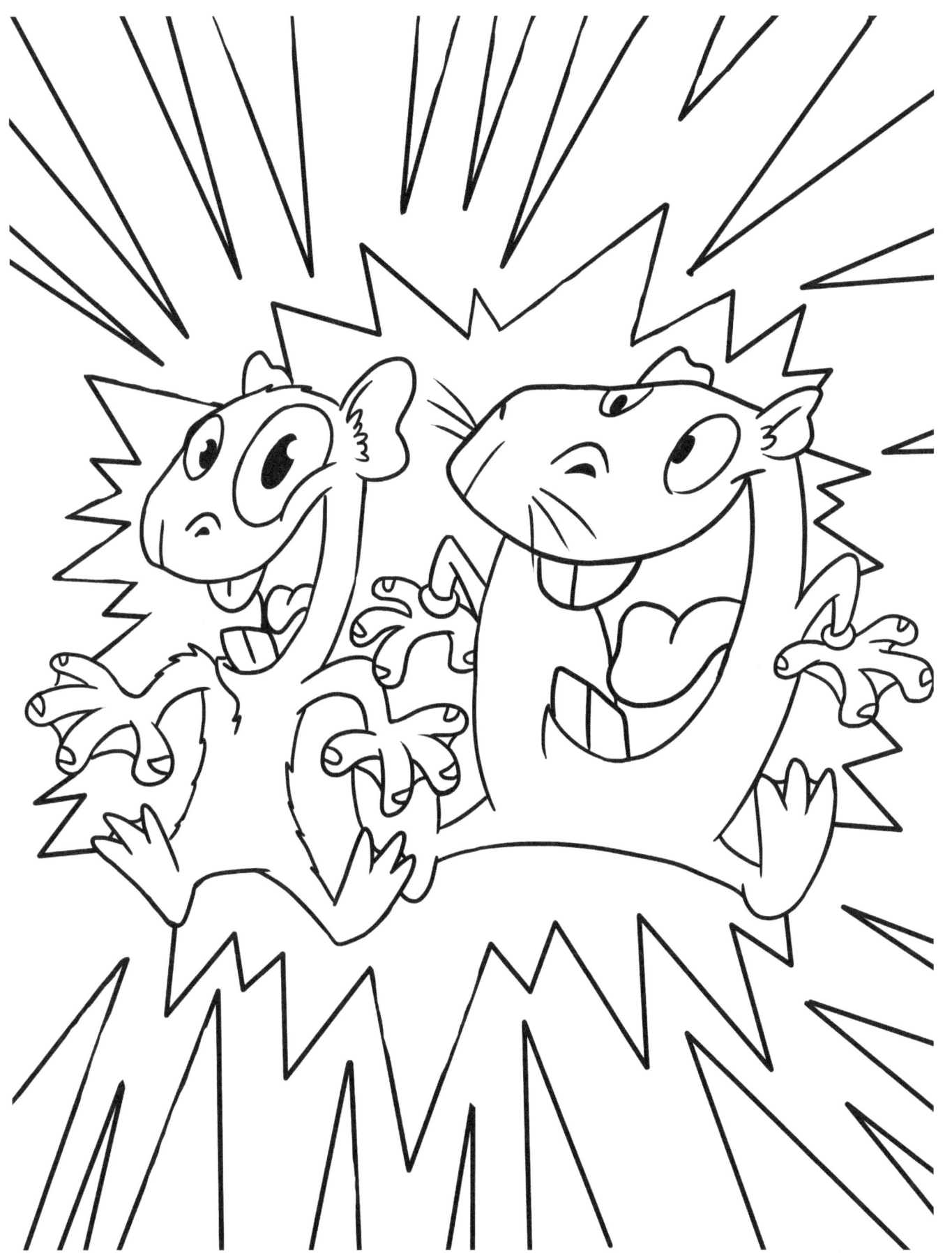

Some groups of capybaras can have up to 100 individual rodents!

Can you find Capy in this photo?

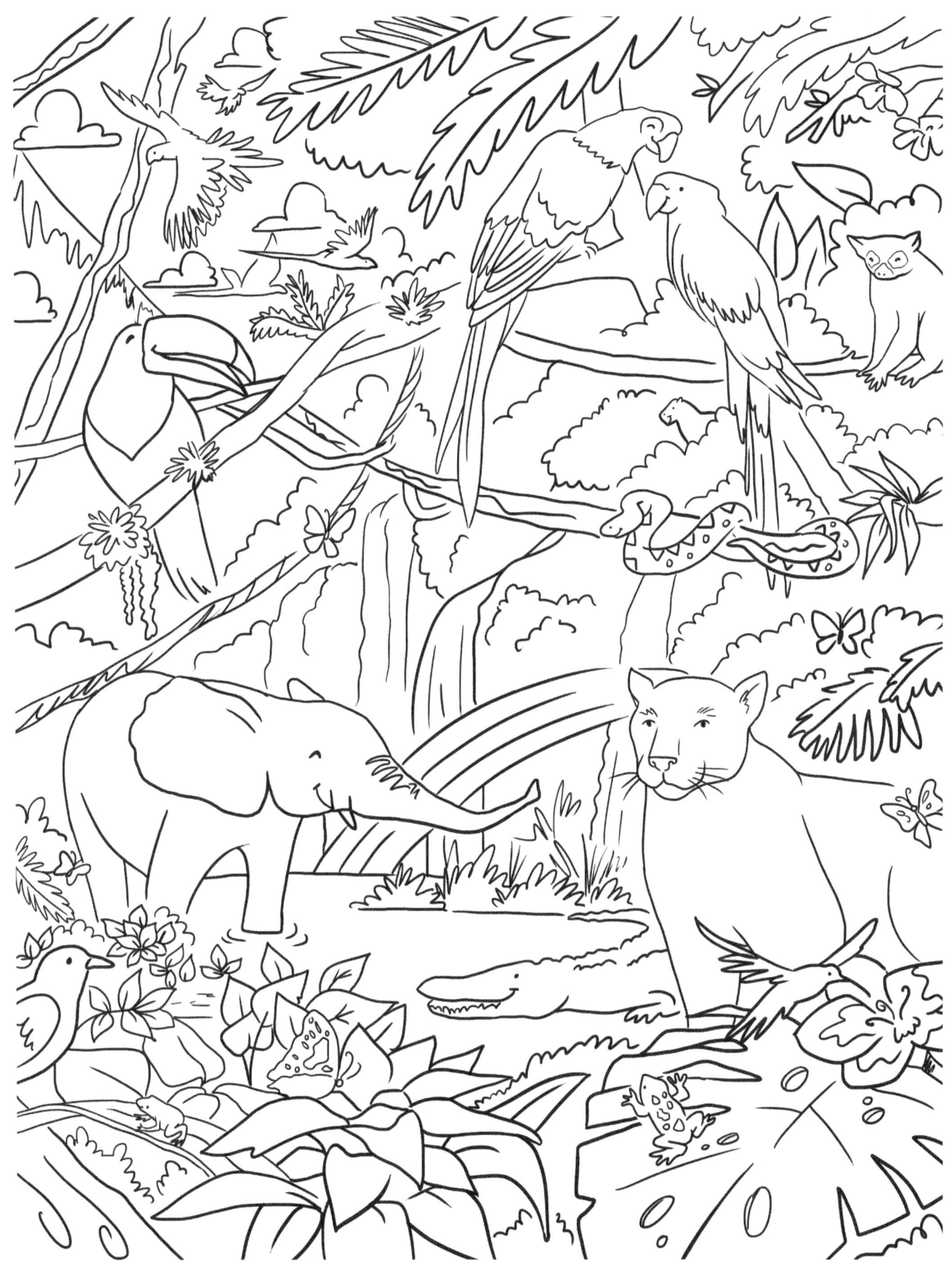

Capybara word search! Let's find some of what we've learned!

Capybara Word Search

U	Y	A	U	G	U	R	U	S	W	A	T	E	R
S	D	N	A	L	G	T	A	E	W	S	I	H	A
R	U	A	R	A	B	Y	P	A	C	S	C	L	M
O	M	H	R	O	H	O	N	C	O	O	H	A	U
H	B	E	R	T	L	P	E	D	R	U	I	N	D
C	N	O	E	A	C	C	I	O	G	T	G	P	E
N	L	E	T	T	L	H	D	U	R	H	U	O	N
I	T	A	H	I	A	E	I	E	E	A	I	T	O
P	O	A	C	H	N	E	T	R	R	M	R	A	S
R	I	K	L	T	S	P	U	P	P	E	E	T	T
A	O	U	W	H	I	S	T	L	E	R	T	O	R
C	A	M	O	R	I	L	L	O	S	I	T	D	I
S	S	I	A	S	E	V	A	E	L	C	P	A	L
S	O	P	P	I	H	L	A	T	N	A	S	G	S

TEETH
LEAVES
RODENT
WHISTLE
SOUTH AMERICA
CHIRP
POTATO
CAPYBARA
CARPINCHO
MORILLOS
WATER
HIPPO
NOSTRILS
CLICK
URUGUAY
MUD
PUPS
CHIGUIRE
SWEAT GLANDS

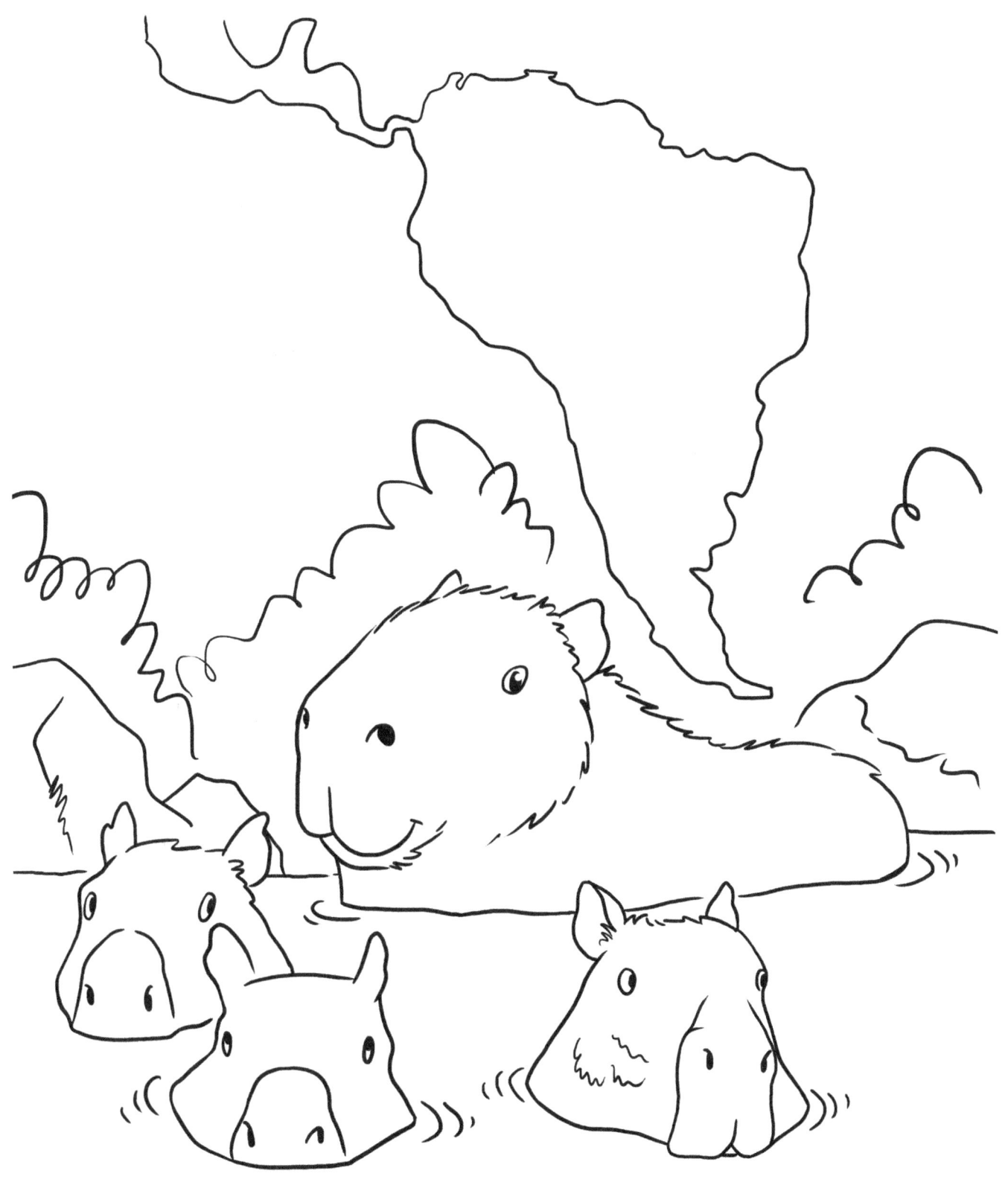

The name "capybara" comes from the Tupi language from Brazil and roughly translates to *one who eats slender leaves*.

In contrast to the leaves, "slender" is not a word often used to describe capybaras, who may eat up to 4 kg (~8 pounds) of grass daily.

Did you eat your vegetables today?

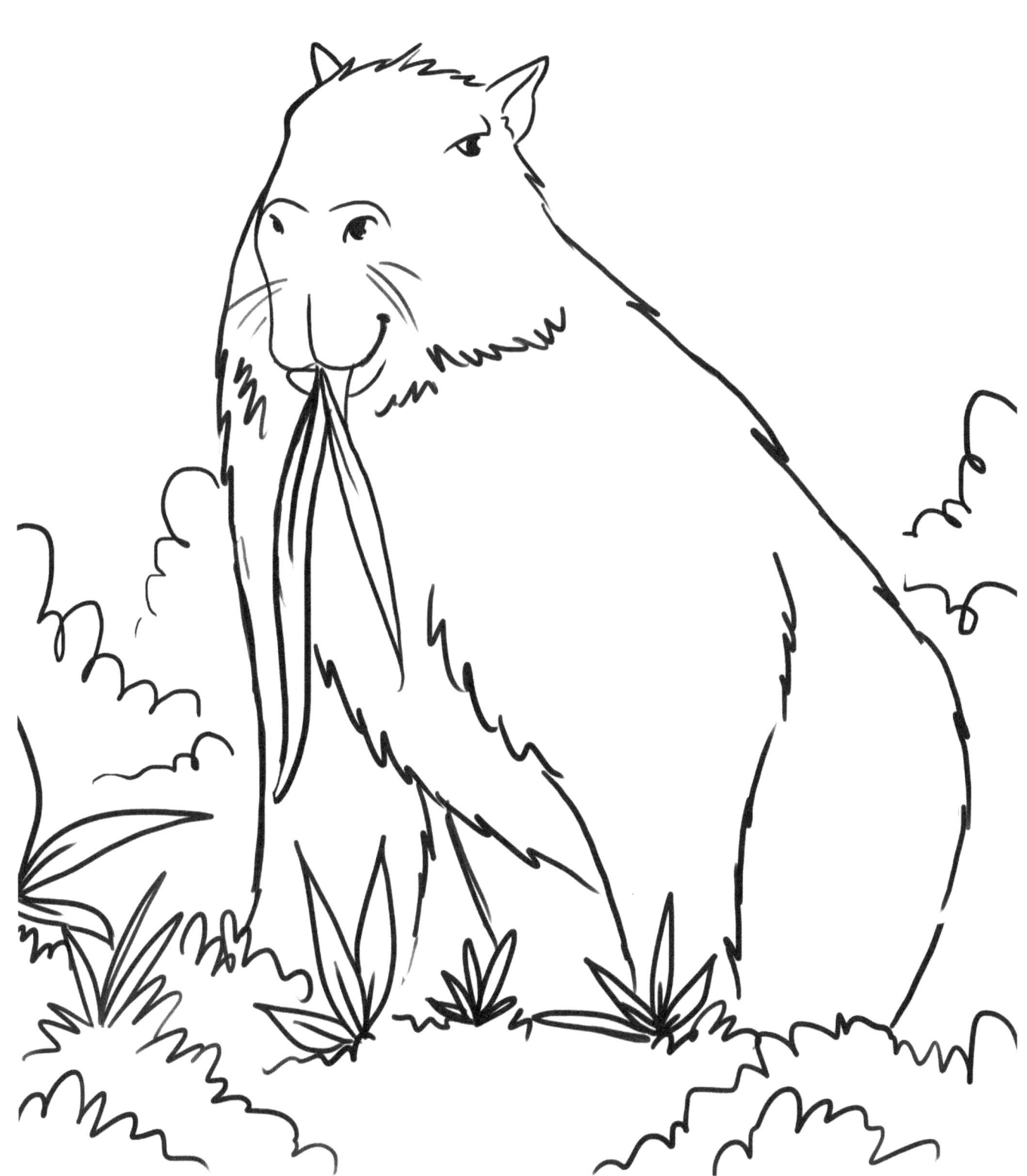

In groups of capybaras, there is usually 1 male for every 4-14 females. Why do you suppose this is?

Wrong answers only.

_____
_____
_____

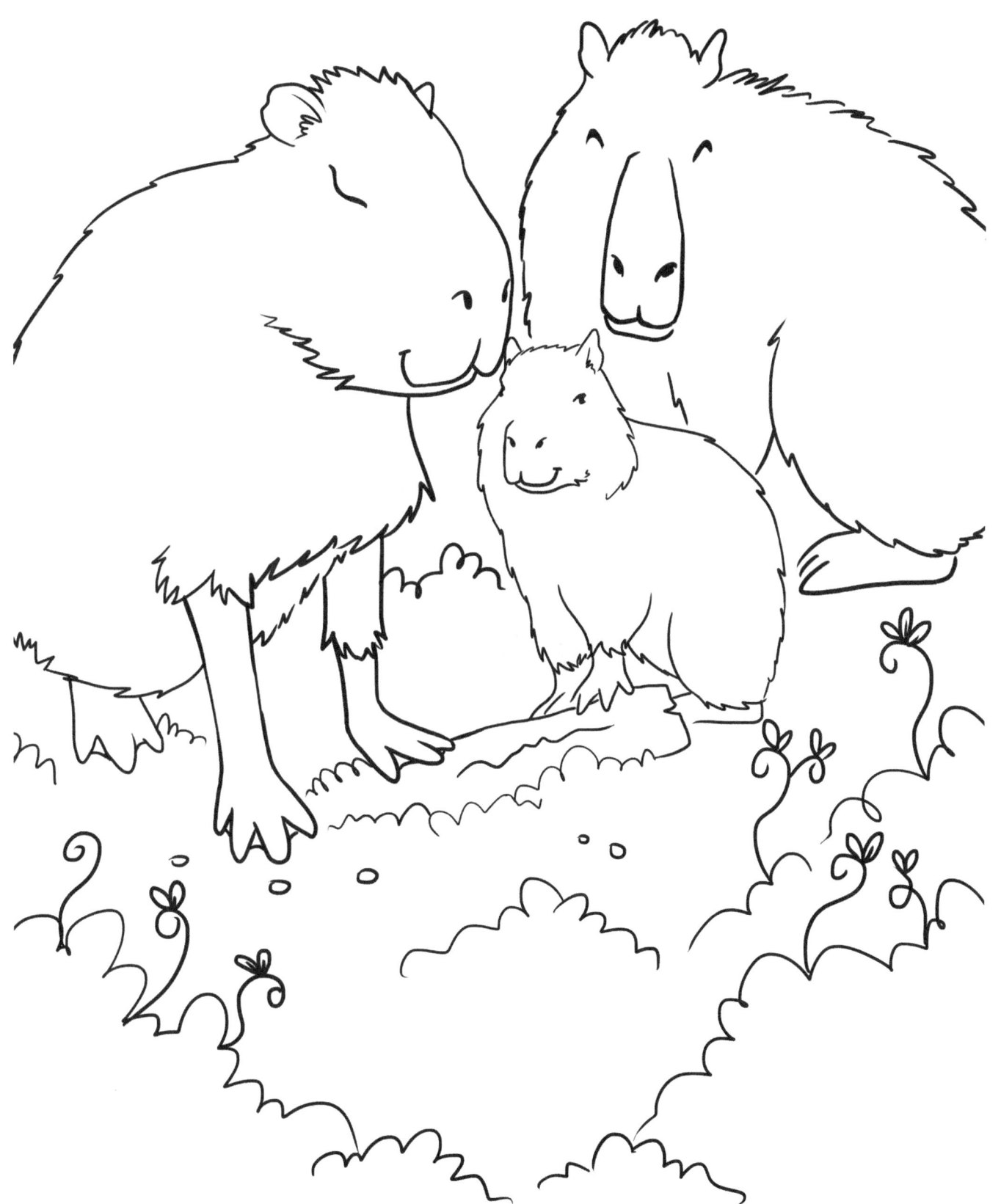

One of my favorite things about capybaras are the noises they make. Seriously, put this book down, and see if you can find a video (or a capybara!) to hear their whistles, purrs, clicks, grunts, and barks.

They are SO expressive!

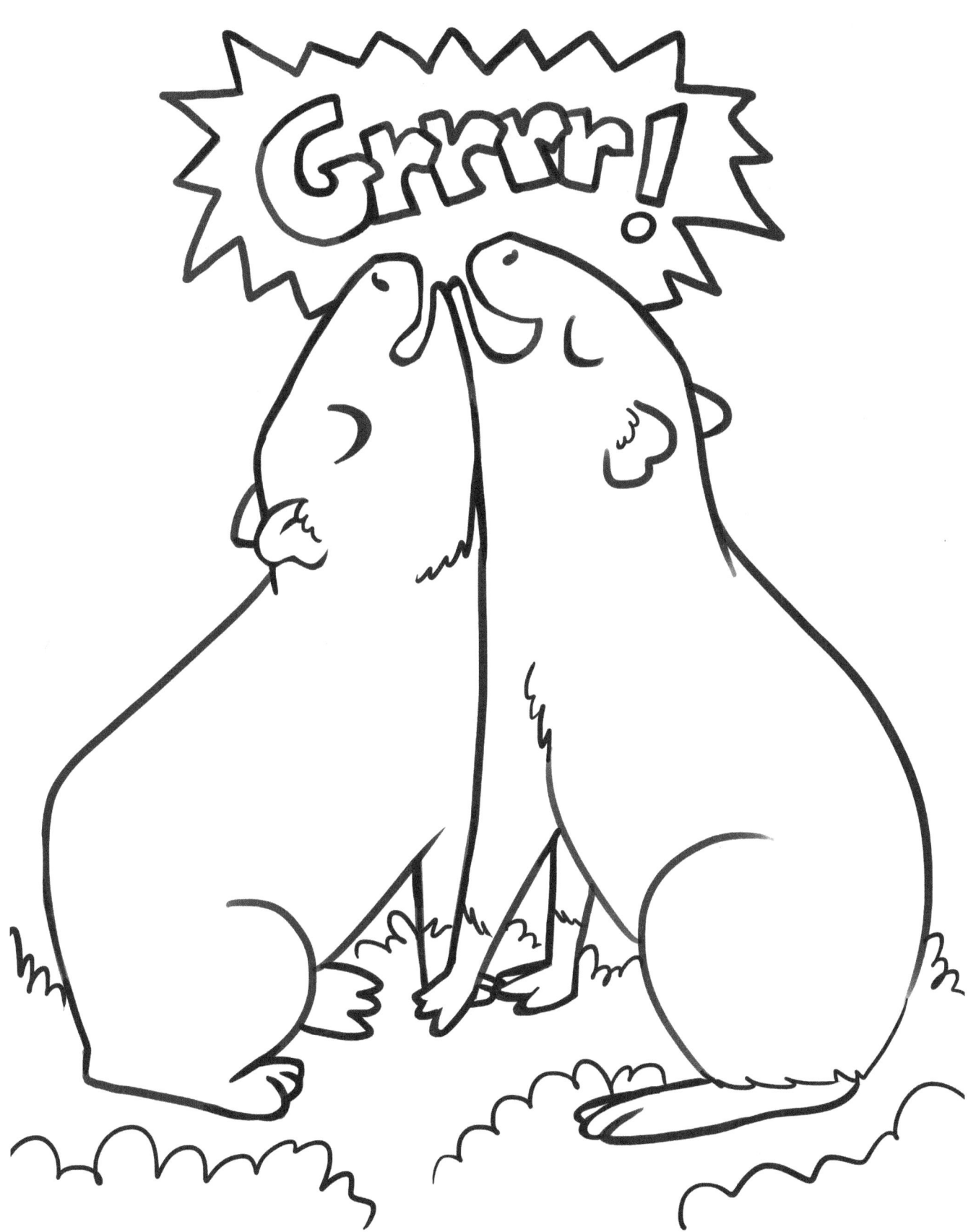

Speaking of expressive, capybaras have special glands in their snouts called "morillos" that they use for leaving their scent on objects, places, and each other.

Sometimes they rub their butts, urinate, or scratch to make sure other capybaras know, "This spot is mine! I was here first".

If you were a capybara, what's the first place, object, person, or animal you would want to declare as exclusively yours?

_____

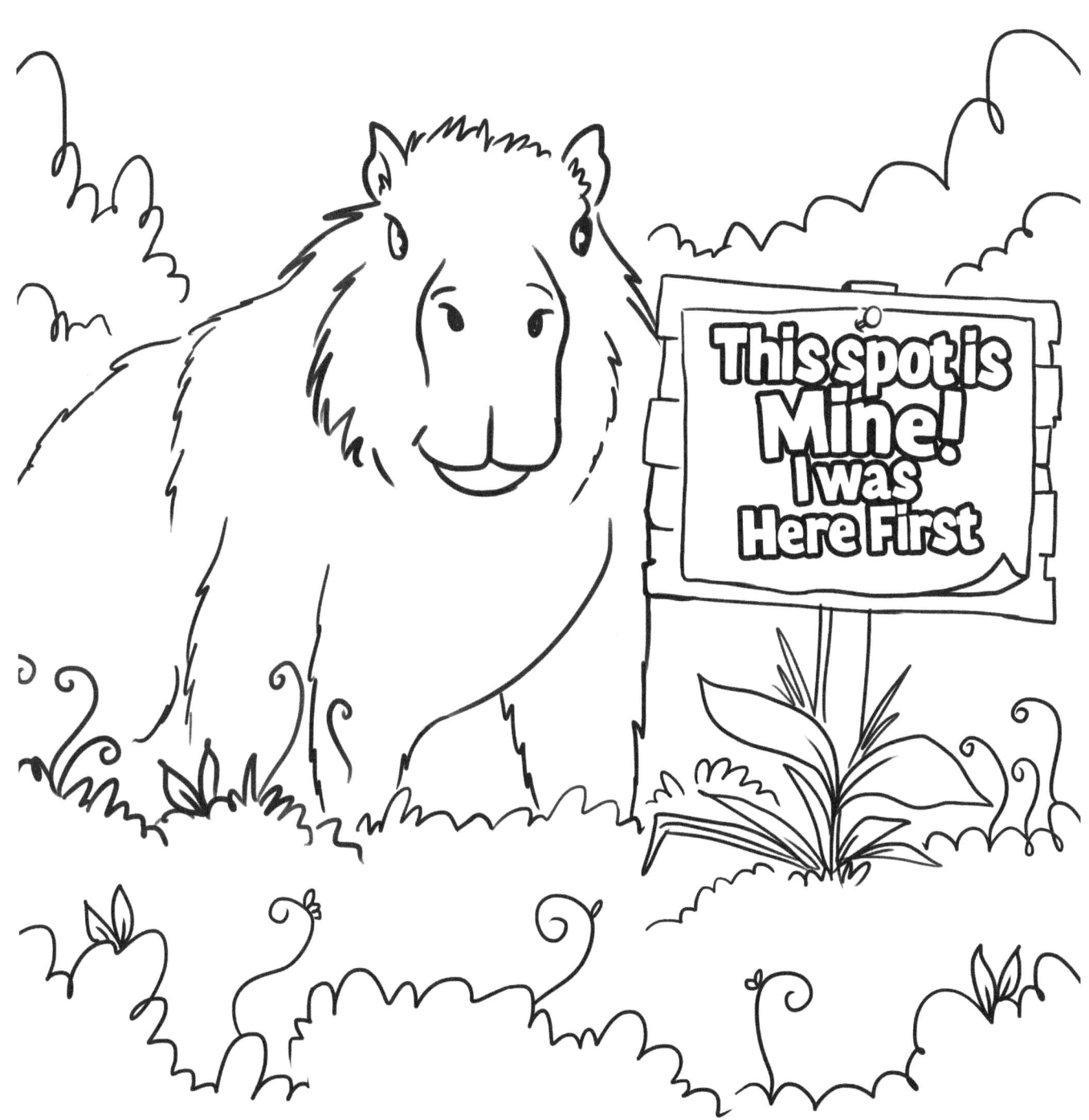

Images of the capybara show up in some really cool places!

- Brazilian currency features the capybara

- Capybaras appear on some wine bottles

- Uruguay has the capybara on their 2 Pesos coin!

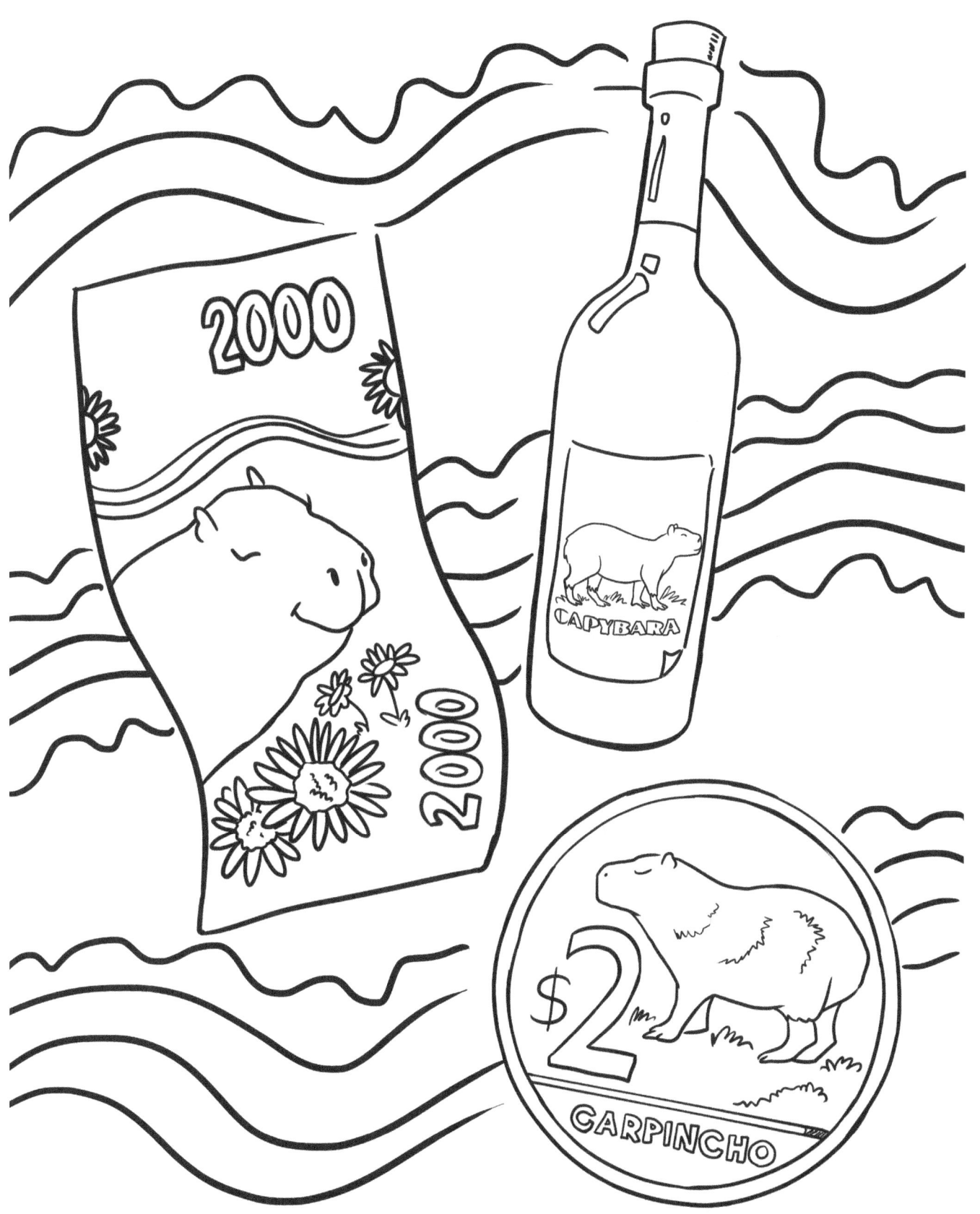

Some other names for the capybara include: chigüire, chigüiro, carpincho, and Bob.

Bob is actually pretty cool and responds to most names as long as you have snacks to share.

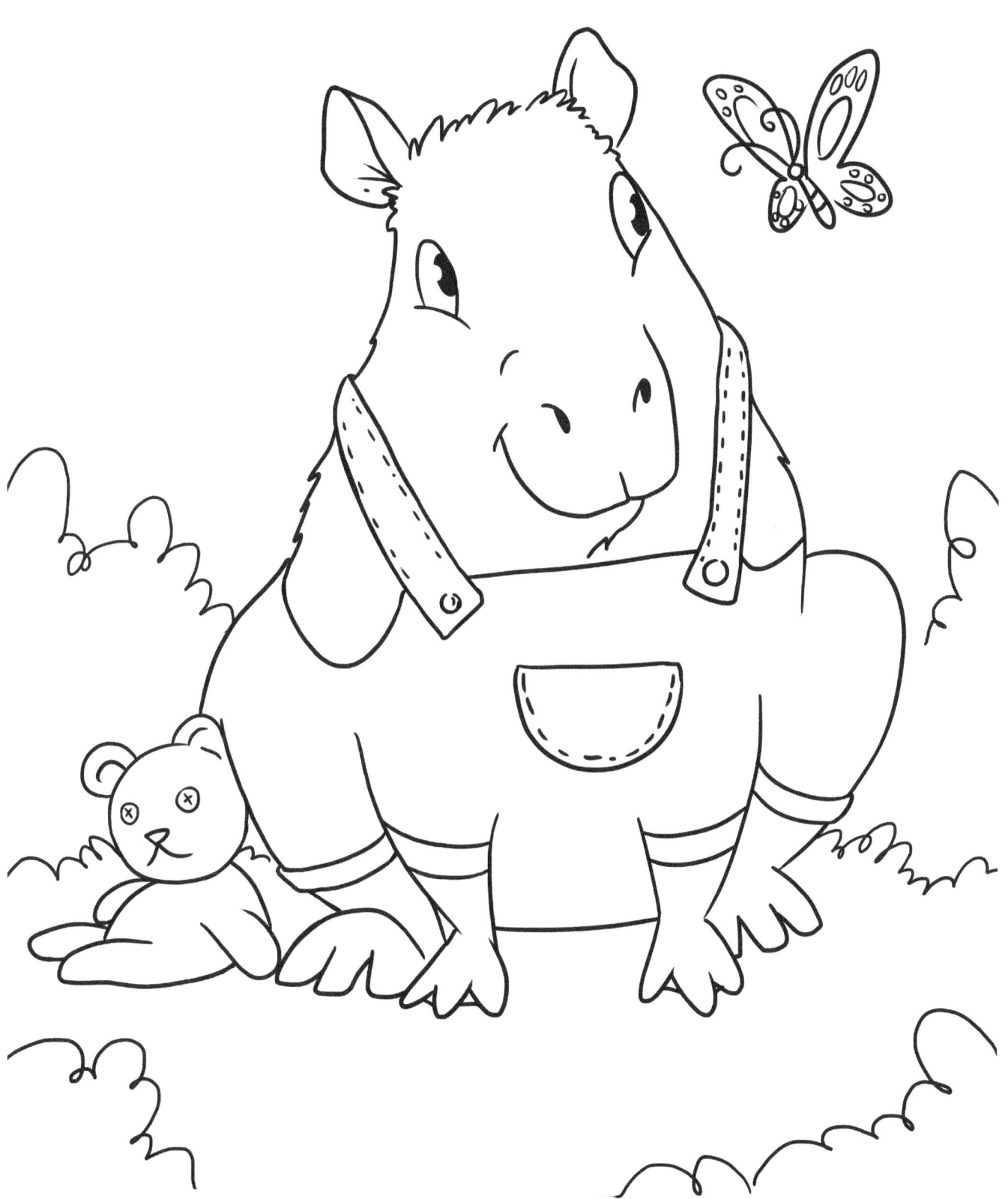

Want to draw a capybara?

Here's the easiest way:

1) Draw a potato*

2) Add legs

3) Add a smile!

***If you don't know how to draw a potato, a delicious burrito works, too.**

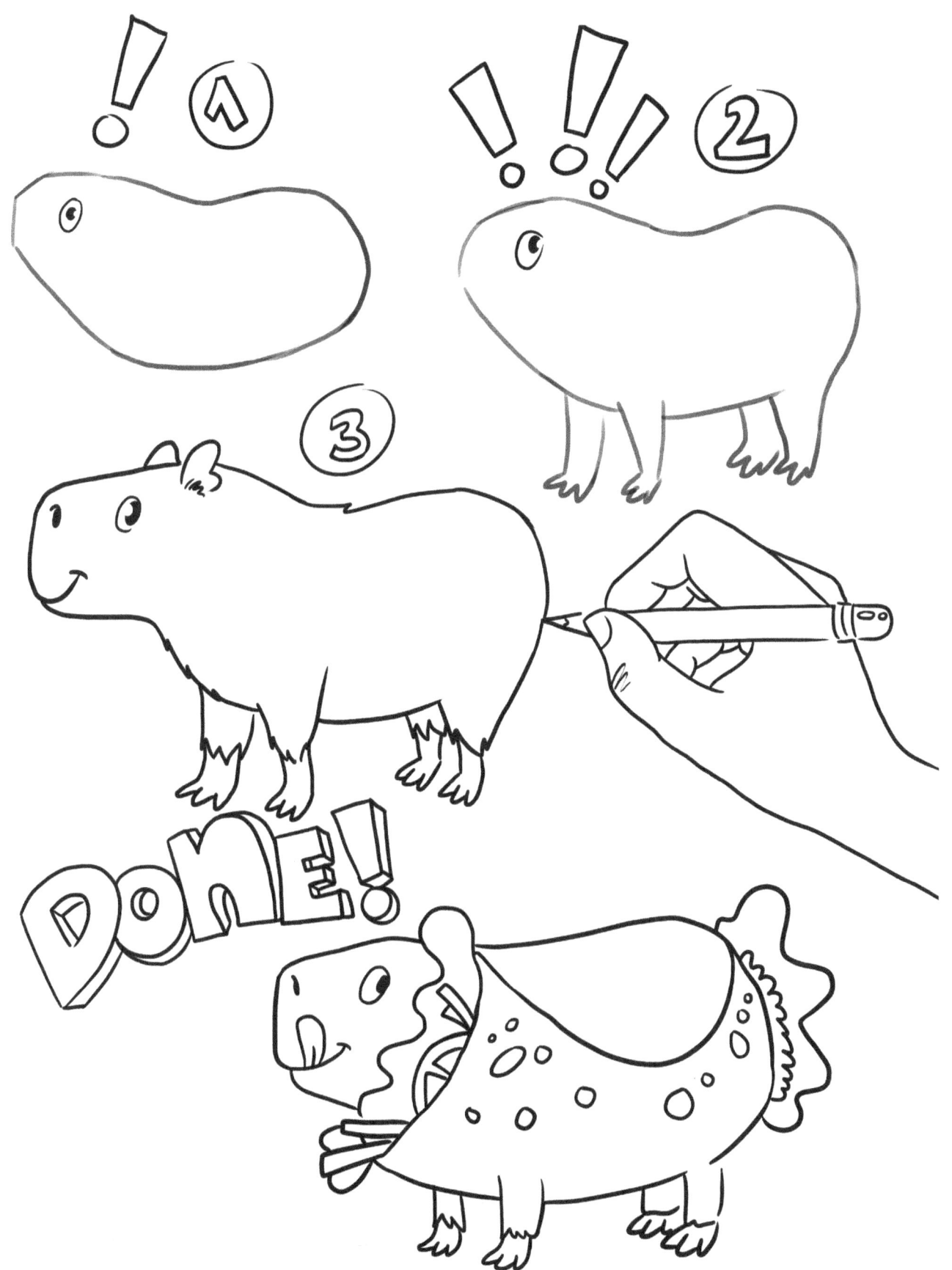

About the Editor

Jonathan Terry, DO, ABIHM, IFMCP is a board-certified osteopathic physician and surgeon, a general psychiatrist, a Diplomate of the American Board of Psychiatry and Neurology (ABPN), a Diplomate of the National Board of Physicians and Surgeons (NBPAS), and a Diplomate of the American Board of Integrative Holistic Medicine (ABIHM). He serves on faculty in several accredited medical schools, residency programs, and professional training programs. Dr. Terry is proud to be a National Health Service Corps Ambassador and works primarily with underserved populations and in consultation for program and policy-building initiatives. Dr. Terry's clinical interests include primary care consultation, nutrition, osteopathy, integrative medicine, kindness, and prevention.

Read more at www.DrJonathanTerry.com, and follow us on Facebook @MyCapybara and @DrJonathanTerry. Dr. Jonathan Terry is also on YouTube.

About the Book

Capy Road is about community investment and involvement at every level. Proceeds from the book are reinvested in local mental health initiatives including prevention, education, and providing free or discounted care to those without insurance, those who cannot access care, students, and impaired professionals.

We're especially proud to feature licensed artwork from *Desiree Albarran* from Bogotá, Colombia. Desiree likes to draw with all possible materials and techniques, making many funny characters that people love. She is a cat lover, cookie hunter, and assiduous gamer. See Desiree's portfolio at: https://www.behance.net/desireeart

For *Capy Road*, we've also enlisted the help of our Layout Editor, Sarah Mugridge. As a true Californian, when she isn't editing capybara coloring books, Sarah can be found soaking up the sunshine outdoors, growing cool plants in her garden, and baking tasty treats!

Finally, we'd like to extend our sincere gratitude and capyness with the many individuals who help to support and share these special books and our mission to help others. You know who you are, and you make us stu-panda-ously, impossibly capy.

Check Out Our Other Colorful Titles:

- *Eat The Rainbow* & the *Eat the Rainbow Coloring Book*
- *The Pursuit of Capyness: A Zen Capybara Coloring Book*
- *Red, White, and Panda: An Educational Red Panda Coloring Book for Adults and Children*
- *Impossibly Opossum: Coloring Book, Facts, and Games!*

IF YOU LIKE THIS BOOK, PLEASE LEAVE US A REVIEW AT YOUR PURCHASE SITE. REVIEWS ARE SO IMPORTANT FOR HELPING THIS BOOK HELP OTHERS